ASIFA

50th ANNIVERSARY

The Animation Art and The History of ASIFA

ASIFA
АСИФА
ASIFA PUBLICATION

www.asifa.net

Association Internationale du Film d'Animation

ASIFA
50th Anniversary Book

ASIFA (Association Internationale du Film d'Animation,
International Animated Film Association)
ASIFA 50th Anniversary book
ISBN 978-89-89488-21-7 03600
2011052500256p

Published by ASIFA™
© Copyright 2011 ASIFA™
All graphic images courtesy of ASIFA's individuals.

Editor in Chief: Ed Desroches
Editors: Nelson Shin, Chris Robinson
Cover design: Nelson Shin
Page design: Nelson Shin, Ed Desroches
Publisher: Nelson Shin
Printed by Hong Dang Moo

Printed in Seoul, Korea

Contents

Looking Forward to Another Half Century of ASIFA

It is with great honour, privilege and joy, that I open this commemorative book with an introduction to celebrate the 50th Anniversary of ASIFA.

It not only marks the five decades of ASIFA's continuous support for the international animation field, but is also a testament to the enduring relevancy of animation in our current world.

The technological and creative advancements of animation have made an organization like ASIFA, a viable, inspirational and collaborative support system for all those who are a part of this very special medium.

This anniversary is especially meaningful to me, as it was 50 years ago that I began in this incredible art form. It has since become my passion to be a part of the work and world of animation. It has been a memorable and deeply meaningful journey for me to witness the growth of this great industry.

clockwise from left
Ed Desroches,
Johnchill Lee,
Vesna Dovnikovic,
Deanna Morse,
Ray Kosarin,
Genevieve Georgesco,
Pencho Kunchev,
Sayoko Kinoshita,
Makiko Nagao,
Oscar Desplats,
David Ehrlich,
Tsvika Oren

ASIFA continues to expand its wings beyond its 32 chapters, with 5500 members in 60 countries worldwide. It continues to promote, protect and support its growing family of animation collaborators and partners around the world.

Festival partners such as Annecy (1960), Zagreb (1972), Ottawa (1976), Cinanima (1977), Hiroshima (1985) and SICAF (1995) have kept the buzz and networking of this industry going strong.

This book will provide a good chance to look back through our short history of a half century. As we look back at the extraordinary last 50 years of ASIFA and its contributions, we can only imagine what further leaps an industry as far-reaching in creative and visionary accomplishments as animation will make in the next 50 years.

Standing at the turning point of ASIFA, I dream that another half of century will be written with more rich and precious fruits in our animation history.

Nelson SHIN

Nelson SHIN is an animation producer, Animator, Chair professor of Bakseok University, CEO of AKOM studios, Editor-in-chief of ANIMATOON, President of ASIFA Korea, President of ASIFA.

Introduction

It is commonly recognized that the 50th year of a company or an association is a very important turning point for its continuation. In order not only to take over the trust and success realized by the ideals and enthusiasms of the founders, as well as to make another new step forward toward the future, it is most essential that the successors have high ambitions as well as passion and courage to act.

When I was elected as the ASIFA President in 2006, I immediately proposed that we publish a special book to record our history precisely, for publication on the occasion of our 50th Anniversary in 2010. As I had good relationships with many of our founders, such as Norman McLaren, Paul Grimault, etc., I thought that it was very important to hand down the strong will and philosophy of our founders to the next generation, just like John Halas and Raoul Servais have done.

Sayoko Kinoshita at Varna 1981.

In the past 50 years it is true that our field of animation art has become very active, however, I regret that the film-makers of animation shorts are still suffering economic hardships. On the other hand, there are numerous animation festivals, from small ones to large ones, around the world, and many filmmakers are desperate to discover as many opportunities as possible by attending those film festivals. Animation filmmakers themselves keep the same enthu-siasms alive as the ASIFA founders, and are taking risks and making efforts to develop the art of animation. As a festival director, I have been meeting and exchanging ideas directly with thousands of filmmakers all over the world for many years, and thus, I have faced their severe situation. I believe it is a very important moment for ASIFA to revive itself as an association that encourages filmmakers and gives them hope. We, meaning ASIFA, must set our future goals earnestly and passionately.

Sayoko Kinoshita

Sayoko Kinoshita is an award winning animation film-maker/producer. With Renzo Kinoshita, she established the Hiroshima Int'l Animation Festival in 1985, and has been serving as the Festival Director since then. ASIFA Vice-President, ASIFA-Japan President, Visiting Professor at Osaka University of Arts.

ASIFA Board Meeting in Annecy '83: Prescott Wright, Bob Balser, Renzo Kinoshita, Hiroko Govarse

It was in 1960 or 1961 I think, that I came across a short insert in the Arts section of the newspaper reporting the creation of an association of animation filmmakers named ASIFA.

I was then a simple provincial amateur filmmaker with no connections to the film business, and I was so thrilled with the news that I immediately wrote to the ASIFA head office in Paris to apply for membership.

ASIFA 50th

Since I was then a beginner with a rather unimpressive résumé, I was afraid it would not be enough to gain me acceptance with the founders of the association. To my great joy however, I soon received the membership card

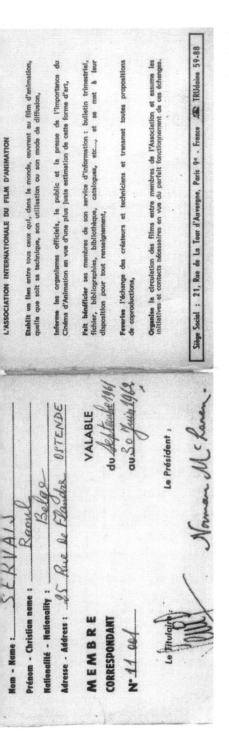

Raoul Servais' first membership card signed by then ASIFA President, Norman McLaren.

I had applied for. Much to my surprise, I first found out that it was signed by ASIFA's first president Norman McLaren; I happened to have shown some of the films of this artist in the film club I had co-founded in Ostend. Then I was surprised to notice that I had been given the membership number 11,001. Back then I thought it indicated that I was now a member of an organization of 11,000, since I appeared to be the 11,001st. I was impressed by numbers akin to those of a military division, and amazed that there were so many animation filmmakers at that time. I learnt later that number 11 was the area code for Belgium, and that number 1 showed that I was the first and only ASIFA member in my own country!

There were not a few thousands of us animated image enthusiasts then; rather a handful, really. It was at the Annecy Film Festival that I met some of ASIFA's founders, whom I later befriended: John Halas, Paul Grimault, Yvan Yvanov Vano, André Martin, Alexandre Alexeieff, Max Massimino Garnier…

Today I am one of those few old-timers of animation who met, at the first film festivals, people who were to become my friends. I can think of Kihachiro Kawamoto, Nag Ansorge, Bretislav Pojar, Fedor Hitruk, Hubert Tison or Frédéric Back. But I have also become very close to "younger" old-timers such as Edward Nazarov, Bruno Bozzeto, Jean-François Laguionie, Jimmy Murakami, Bordo Dovnikovic, Jerzy Kucia, Michel Ocelot, Daniel Szschecura, Sayoko Kinoshita, Manuel Otero, and many others.

In 1985, I was so allergic to administrative duties that it took all of John Halas's persuasion to convince me to take over from him as ASIFA president. But I would not have made it through those nine years of bureaucratic hard work without the unmatched efforts of general secretary Nicole Salomon. It is her dedication, competence, impartiality and intransigence that have enabled me to do well in my three

Upper left: ASIFA Board Meeting in Annecy '81.
Upper right: From left Nicole Salomon, Raha Abyaneh, Raoul Servais, Nourredin ZarrinKelk, Buba Antauer, Bretislav Pojar, Michael Dudok DeWit at Zagreb Animation Festival 1996.
Above: Raoul Servais.

successive terms as international president. An animation-lover, she was not only involved in the foundation of the Annecy Film Festival and the growth of ASIFA, but she also won the friendship and gratitude of many animated film artists.

I have always been impressed by the surprising team spirit that prevailed among ASIFA members. In the difficult years of the Cold War, people in international meetings would fear, insult and threaten one another; there never was such behaviour within our organization, quite the contrary: many friendships grew in spite of iron curtains.
Over the years, the successive international presidents of ASIFA have hailed from America, Europe and Asia. Let us hope that with the animation bug now apparently biting in Africa and Oceania as well, the torch will soon be passed on to members from these two continents.

Although ASIFA's initiatives have greatly encouraged the art of animation and enabled hundreds of independent film-makers from around the world to meet, bring their work to the public and, thanks to its publications, keep to the path of animation, we still have a long way to go.

While it is true that for the past few years, the number of animated features has increased, their quality has improved, and the format has found new markets in theatres as well as television, animated shorts, which are mainly the works of independent artists, are still too rarely seen. And yet, making due allowance, we can undoubtedly claim that there are more masterpieces to be found among short films than feature films—which is quite natural since short film directors are less dependent on economic factors.

There aren't enough art museums, community arts centres, libraries or video libraries acquainted with auteur animated films. But public institutions of the kind should be able to

Four ASIFA presidents: Raoul Servais, Noureddin ZarrinKelk, Nelson Shin, Sayoko Kinoshita at Hiroshima Animation Festival closing ceremonies 2010.

Zagreb '88: ASIFA Board Meeting.

Hiroshima '92: Picnic:
Georges Lacroix, Nicole
Salomon, Menno de Nooijer,
Petra Freeman, Michele
Cournoyer, Peter Dougherty,
Phillip Hunt, Thomas
Renoldner, Tim Rolt.

make up for the poor circulation of such films for lack of specialized theatres and television programs. It seems to me that this must be one of ASIFA's present priorities.

Since our association lives on its members' modest subscriptions alone, it is plain for all to see that informational and promotional efforts cannot be conducted on a worldwide scale. But those of national or regional ASIFA chapters in constant and dynamic operation should tell the international board of directors what cultural centres in their area have to offer.

No association will be dynamic unless new members regularly come to swell its ranks. ASIFA is aware of this and sets up booths and talks in some international animation film festivals in order to make itself known to prospective members.

However, with such a great number of colleges of animation and higher education institutes, it might be worthwhile if each national or regional chapter sent out a delegate to these schools to draw the attention of future professionals to ASIFA.

Top: Annie Maillet(the lady turned sideways),
Raoul Servais (middle) and Pierre Vlerik(right side).
Bottom: Across from the Hiroshima Animation
Festival impromptu jam sessions start up at Otis' Bar.

And if we could afford it, it would of course be advisable for the international board of directors to appoint someone qualified and multilingual as ASIFA "ambassador" to cultural centres and schools in every country where animation is growing significantly.

It has been some time since I was an executive member of ASIFA, and I might have just stated the obvious here and there. But be assured that all that I have said up until now stems from a true devotion to the cause of animation.

Raoul Servais

Raoul Servais is a great master of animation. Belgian pioneer of animated films and founder of KASK,the first school for animation in Europe. He is best known as maker of some twelve animated films, which won him several prizes at most major international film festivals.

Translation: Pauline Drapeau, AFCA/ASIFA France
Proofreading: Madeleine Laurencin

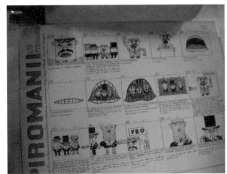

Some of the original artwork for various animations can be found at A.A.A. a children's animation workshop studio in Annecy, France.

Preface

I have to confess – and it doesn't make me proud – that I did not watch cartoons in my youth and that until my early 20s I had no interest in doing so. What happened then was my encounter with ASIFA. It was a new world, cinematically speaking, and a very welcoming world. A new family, almost.

October, 1969 : After an ASIFA Meeting this picture was taken on the Baker Street film set at Pinewood Film Studios - home of Sherlock Holmes. Front row from left: John Halas (UK), Fedor Khitruk (USSR), Gunnar Karlssen (Sweden), Max Massimino Garnier & wife (Italy), Gyula Macskassy (Hungary), Francoise Jaubert (Canada), Gyorgy Matolcsy (Hungary), Joachim Kreck's partner (UK), Ivan Ivanov-Vano (USSR), Clare Kitson (UK), Joachim Kreck (W. Germany), Annie Debilde, Interpreter, Sandy Fleet (USA West). Middle Row: Manuel Otero's partner (France), Todor Dinov (Bulgaria), Katja Georgi (East Germany), Jerzy Kotowski (Poland), Bruno Edera(Switzerland), Manuel Otero (France). Back row: Dick Rauh (USA East)

I had recently graduated in modern languages and taken a day job which bored me to tears. But I inherited from a university friend a post assisting John Halas, one evening a week, on his ASIFA correspondence, much of which was in French. I was hooked. Suddenly I was watching animated films at every opportunity and trying to read in them the coded thoughts of filmmakers from far-flung lands. These were interesting times for the organization, after the events of 1968 had led to the French government cancelling its subsidy to ASIFA along with that year's Annecy festival. John was called on to step in, to look for support elsewhere, to enliven the image of animation around the world and to foster international animated connections.

John was one of a kind. He could be exasperating – but what a powerhouse. What a huge investment in time, energy and what I suspect was his own money, to nurture that fledgling network. In 1969 he brought ASIFA representatives from around the world to a summit in London to discuss solutions. There I met animators, distributors, studio heads, historians, all utterly committed to animation and to ASIFA. Then, thanks to an encounter at the Mamaia (Romania) festival in 1970, I was able to leave the boring London day job for a stint in Los Angeles, assembling animation programmes, working with ASIFA stalwarts such as June Foray, Bill Littlejohn, Bill Hurtz, Prescott Wright

Left: From left Bill Hurtz, unidentified, Boris Kolar, Mrs Hurtz, June Foray, Zdenka Deitchova, Gene Deitch, Clare Kitson enjoying the day in Annecy 1973.
Right: Kecskemet 1985 - John Halas being interviewed

Top from left: Normand Roger,
Alexandre Petrov,
Noureddin ZarrinKelk,
Marcy Page and Alik Shpiluyk
at the KROK festival 2005.

Left clockwise: Ed Desroches,
Nelson Shin,
Noureddin ZarrinKelk,
Deanna Morse, Juliette Crochu,
and Anastasia Dimitra

Below: Happy New Year Greeting
by Noureddin Zarrinkelk.

and Les Goldman, and acting as US west coast coordinator for the first Zagreb festival (1972). I couldn't believe my luck when it transpired that this involved working with the 'fathers' who were to be celebrated by retrospectives there: Chuck Jones, Friz Freleng, Dave Fleischer, Walter Lantz…

Throughout the period I was sometimes asked to help at international board meetings, sometimes taking minutes, sometimes (inexpertly) interpreting, and thus witnessing Cold War relationships up close. Despite mutual suspicion and frequent high drama, agreements were slowly thrashed out, film exchanges, visiting delegations and new festivals organized.

Later, working for the British Film Institute, I would encounter filmmakers from the 'real' world of live action, which only confirmed my conviction that animators regardless of their geographic origins are, alongside their huge talent, by and large more modest, eccentric, witty, perceptive and nice to be with. It was ASIFA which set me on my course, programming, commissioning and writing about animation – and for this I'll always be very, very grateful.

Clare Kitson

Clare Kitson commissioned animation for Britain's Channel 4 Television in the 90s. She is now a free-lance writer, programmer and translator.

ASIFA Board meeting HIROSHIMA 1996
From left: unidentified, Renzo Kinoshita, Gerben Schermer, Pat Raine Webb, David Ehrlich, Vesna & Bordo Dovnikovic, Otto Alder, Thomas Renoldner.

President: John Hubley, USA
Vice-Presidents: Ivan Ivanov Vano, USSR, Vojen Masnik, Czechoslovakia,
        Jurica Peruzovic, Yugoslavia, Ian Popescu Gopo, Romania
Secretary General: Pierre Barbin, France
Treasurer: John Halas, UK
Board Members: Norman McLaren, Canada, Ryszard Brudzynski, Poland, Robert Cannon, USA
        Ezio Gagliardo, Italy, Paul Grimault, France, Stig Lasseby, Sweden

President: Pierre Barbin, France
Honorary Presidents: Norman McLaren, Canada, John Hubley, USA
Vice Presidents: Ivan Ivanov Vano , USSR, William Littlejohn, USA, Ion Popescu Gopo, Romania
        Vojen Masnik, Czechoslovakia
Secretary General &Treasurer: Marin Paraianu, Romania
Board Members: Yoji Kuri, Japan, Paul Grimault, France, Ezio Gagliardo, Italy
        Max Massimino Garnier, Italy, Nikola Kostelac, Yugoslavia
        Jerzy Kotowski, Poland, Robert Verral, Canada

President: Francoise Jaubert, Canada
Vice-Presidents: John Halas, UK, Ivan Ivanov Vano, USSR
        William Littlejohn, USA, Ion Popescu Gopo, Romania
Secretary General: Marin Paraianu, Romania
Treasurer: Zelimir Matko, Yugoslavia
Board Members: Lev Atamanov, USSR, Jiri Brdecka, Czechoslovakia
        Todor Dinov, Bulgaria, Ezio Gagliardo, Italy, Les Goldman, USA
        Max Massimino Garnier, Italy, Jerzy Kotowsky, Poland
        Yoji Kuri, Japan, Raymond Maillet, France, Gyorgy Matolcsy, Hungary
        Manuel Otero, France, Milivoj Pogrmilovic, Yugoslavia, Robert Verrall, Canada

President: Pierre Barbin, France
Honorary Presidents: Norman McLaren, Canada, John Hubley, USA
Vice Presidents: Ivan Ivanov Vano, USSR, William Littlejohn, USA
        Ion Popescu Gopo, Romania, Vojen Masnik, Czechoslovakia
Secretary General &Treasurer: Marin Paraianu, Romania
Board Members: Yoji Kuri, Japan, Paul Grimault, France, Ezio Gagliardo, Italy
        Max Massimino Garnier, Italy, Nikola Kostelac, Yugoslavia
        Jerzy Kotowski, Poland, Robert Verral, Canada

50 YEARS OF ASIFA

| 1956 | 1957 | 1958 | 1959 | 1960 | 1961 | 1962 | 1963 | 1964 | 1965 | 1966 | 1967 | 1968 | 1969 | 1970 | 1971 | 1972 |

ASIFA was offcially declared an association.
It was registered in France on June 15, 1961.

First international animation festival in the world
specialized for animation is held in Annecy, France from 7-12 June.
In Italy that same year, the draft structure of
ASIFA is drawn up, with Norman McLaren as its President.

In a second meeting, the participants include Norman McLaren, Jiri Trnka,
Alexandre Alexeie, John Hubley, Paul Grimault, Ivan Ivanov Vano, and others.
Concrete plans for the foundation of ASIFA.

During the 9th Cannes Film Festival run the first initatives for the foundation
of an international animation association.

President: Francoise Jaubert, Canada
Vice-Presidents: Paul Grimault, France, William Littlejohn, USA
                 Ion Poposcu Gopo, Romania, Boris Stepantsev, USSR
Secretary General: György Matolcsy, Hungary
Treasurer: Milivoj Pogrmilovic, Yugoslavia
Board Members: Lev Atamanov, USSR, Jiri Brdecka, Czechoslovakia, Todor Dinov, Bulgaria
                Ezio Gagliardo, Italy, Max Massimino Garnier, Italy, Katja Georgi, GDR
                Les Goldman, USA, John Halas, Great Britain, Marcell Jankovics, Hungary
                Rene Jodoin, Canada, Jerzy Kotowsky, Poland, Raymond Maillet, France
                Zelimir Matko, Yugoslavia, Yoji Kuri, Japan, Karel Zeman, Czechoslovakia

President: John Halas, UK
Vice-Presidents: Max Massimino Garnier, Italy, Paul Grimault, France
                 William Littlejohn, USA, Boris Stepancev, USSR
Secretary General: György Matolcsy, Hungary
Treasurer: Milivoj Pogrmilovic, Yugoslavia
Board Members: Lev Atamanov, USSR, Stojan Dukov, Bulgaria, Katja Georgi, GDR
                Bob Godfrey, UK, Les Goldman, USA, Marcell Jankovics, Hungary
                Francoise Jaubert, Canada, Kihachiro Kawamoto, Japan, Jerzy Kotowsky, Poland
                Raymong Maillet, France, Zelimir Matko, Yugoslavia, Inni Karine Melbye, Norvay
                Ion Popescu Gopo, Romania, Zdenek Smetana, Czechoslovakia, Aldo Raparelli, Italy

President: John Halas, UK
Vice-Presidents: Max Massimino Garnier, Italy, Katja Georgi, GDR
                 Bill Littlejohn, USA, Boris Stepancev, USSR
General Secretary: György Matolcsy, Hungary
Treasurer: Zelimir Matko, Yugoslavia
Board Members: Lev Atamanov, USSR, Bob Balser, USA, Borivoj Dovnikovic, Yugoslavia
                Stoyan Dukov, Bulgaria, Bob Godfrey, UK, Les Goldman, USA
                Ion Popescu Gopo, Romania, Co Hoedeman, Canada, Marcell Jankovics, Hungary
                Kihachiro Kawamoto, Japan, Jerzy Kotowski, Poland, Derek Lamb, Canada
                Inni Karine Melbye, Norway, Aldo Raparelli, Italy, Nicole Salomon, France

President: John Halas, UK
Vice-Presidents: Katja Georgi, GDR, Max Garnier, Italy
                 Bill Littlejohn, USA, Boris Stepancev, USSR
Secretary General: György Matolcsy, Hungary
Treasurer: Vladimir Goldman
Board Members: Bob Balser, USA, Peter Brouwer, Netherlands, Borivoj Dovnikovic, Yugoslavia
                Stoyan Dukov, Bulgaria, Bob Godfey, UK, Ion Popescu Gopo, Romania
                Feodor Khitruk, USSR, Renzo Kinoshita, Japan, Inni Karine Melbye, Norway
                Kelly O'Brien, Canada, Huguette Parent, Canada, Nicole Salomon, France
                Veronique Steeno, Belgium, Daniel Szczechura, Poland, Prescott Wright, USA

1974	1975	1976	1977	1978	1979	1980	1981	1982	1983	1984	1985

The head office was transfered from Paris to the Annecy Hotel de Ville.
The organizing of ASIFA Committee No. 5 was formed on Workshops with Nicole Salomon as its President.

ASIFA installs the ASIFA Prize. The ASIFA Prize is awarded annually to individuals or organisations which have made a signifcant and innovative contribution towards the promotion and preservation of the art of animation.

President: John Halas, UK
Vice-Presidents: Feodor Khitruk, USSR, Nicole Salomon, France
                 Prescott Wright, USA, Daniel Szczechura, Poland
Secretary General: Peter Tiborsky, Hungary
Treasurer: Huguette Parent, Canada
Board Members: György Matolcsy, Hungary, Renzo Kinoshita, Japan, Bob Balser, USA
                Kelly O'Brian, Canada, Adrian Petringenaru, Romania, Vadim Kurchevsky, USSR
                Bob Godfrey, UK, Ranko Munitic, Yugoslavia, Giannalberto Bendazzi, Italy
                Veronique Steeno, Belgium, Inni Karine Melbye, Norway, Stoyan Dukov, Bulgaria
                Max Massimino Garnier, Italy, Gustav Verspeelt, Belgium

President: Raoul Servais, Belgium
Vice-Presidents: Bob Balser, USA, Howard Beckerman, USA
                 Feodor Khitruk, USSR, Renzo Kinoshita, Japan
Secretary General: Nicole Salomon, France
Treasurers: Jiri Kubicek, Czechoslovakia, Antti Peranne, Finland
Board Members: Giannalberto Bendazzi, Italy, Stoyan Dukov, Bulgaria, Bob Godfrey, UK
                Jerzy Kucia, Poland, Bill Littlejohn, USA, Nikola Majdak, Yugoslavia
                György Matolcsy, Hungary, Inni Karine Melbye, Norway, Kelly O'Brian, Canada
                Adrian Peringenaru, Romania, Veronique Steeno, Belgium, Kurt Weller, GDR
                Xu Jing Da, China, Yitzak Yoresh, Israel

President: Raoul Servais, Belgium
Vice-Presidents: Renzo Kinoshita, Japan, Bob Balser, USA
                 Eduard Nazarov, USSR, Howard Beckerman, USA
Secretary General: Nicole Salomon, France
Treasurers: Antti Peranne, Finland, Jiri Kubicek, Czechoslovakia
Board Members: Giannalberto Bendazzi, Italy, David Ehrlich, USA, Jerzy Kucia, Poland
                Kati Macskassy, Hungary, Nikola Majdak, Yugoslavia, Priit Pärn, USSR
                Veronique Steeno, Belgium, Gunnar Strøm, Norway, Helene Tanguay, Canada
                Pat Raine Webb, UK, Kurt Weller, GDR, Yan Ding Xian, China
                Yitzak Yoresh, Israel, Noureddin Zarrinkelk, Iran

President: Raoul Servais, Belgium
Vice-Presidents: David Ehrlich, USA, Renzo Kinoshita, Japan
                 Eduard Nazarov, Russia, Pat Raine Webb, UK
Secretary General: Gunnar Strøm, Norway
Treasurer: Lennart Spindler, Sweden
Board Members: Otto Alder, Germany, Bob Balser, USA, Yan Ding Xian, China
                Robi Engler, Switzerland, Jiri Kubicek, Czech Republic, Jerzy Kucia, Poland
                Marty McNamara, USA, Nikola Majdak, Serbia, Michel Ocelot, France
                Priit Pärn, Estonia, Helene Tanguay, Canada, Yitzak Yoresh, Israel

President: Michel Ocelot, France
Vice-Presidents: David Ehrlich, USA, Renzo Kinoshita, Japan
                 Jerzy Kucia, Poland, Eduard Nazarov, Russia
Secretary General: Borivoj Dovnikovic, Croatia
Treasurer: Huguette Parent, Canada
Board Members: Otto Alder, Germany, Yan Ding Xian, China, Robi Engler, Switzerland
                Jiri Kubicek, Czech Republic, Martin McNamara, USA, Thomas Renoldner, Austria
                Normand Roger, Canada, Gerben Schermer, Netherlands, Gunnar Strøm, Norway
                Pat Raine Webb, UK, Noureddin Zarrinkelk, Iran

1986	1987	1988	1989	1990	1991	1992	1993	1994	1995	1996	1997	1998	1999	2000

President: Michel Ocelot, France
Vice-Presidents: Sayoko Kinoshita, Japan, Normand Roger, Canada
                 Gunnar Strøm, Norway,
Secretary General: Borivoj Dovnikovic, Croatia
Treasurer: Ton Crone, The Netherlands
Board Members: Pierre Azuelos, France, David Ehrlich, USA, Abi Fejo, Portugal
                Jiri Kubicek, Czech Republic, Jerzy Kucia, Poland, Ferenc Mikulas, Hungary
                Deanna Morse, USA, Jin Guo Ping, China, Jonas Raeber, Switzerland
                Thomas Renoldner, Austria, Hubert Tison, Canada
                Stanislav Ulver, Czech Republic, Noureddin Zarrinkelk, Iran

President: Abi Fejo, Portugal till 2001
          Thomas Renoldner, Austria 02-03
Vice-Presidents: Marco de Blois, Canada, Sayoko Kinoshita, Japan
          Antran Manoogian, USA, Andy Wyatt, UK
Secretary General: Vesna Dovnikovic, Croatia
Members: Wendy Jackson Hall, USA, Heikki Jokinen, Finland
          Thomas Renoldner, Austria, Chris Robinson, Canada

President: Noureddin Zarrinkelk, Iran
Vice Presidents: Sayoko Kinoshita, Japan, Antran Manoogian, USA
          Thomas Renoldner, Austria
Secretary General: Vesna Dovnikovic
Treasurer: Carol Beecher, Canada 03-04
          Thomas Renoldner 04-06

President: Sayoko Kinoshita, Japan
Vice Presidents: Deanna Morse, USA, Nelson Shin, Korea
          Antran Manoogian, USA, Pencho Kunchev, Bulgaria
Secretary General: Vesna Dovnikovic, Croatia
Treasurer: Thomas Renoldner, Austria

President: Nelson Shin, Korea
Vice Presidents: Sayoko Kinoshita, Japan, Antran Manoogian, USA
          Ed Desroches, USA, Heikki Jokinen, Finland
Secretary General: Vesna Dovnikovic, Croatia
Treasurer: Anastasia Dimitra, Greece
Executive Director: Bill Dennis, India (for onel year of trial period)

2001 2002 2003 2004 2005 2006 2007 2008 2009 2010 2011 2012

The position of the ASIFA Executive Director has been inaugurated.

ASIFA has more than 5.000 members on all continents and 32 national chapters
in Europe, Asia, Africa, North and South America.

Change of the ASIFA structure, new ASIFA Statutes.
There are no elections for the ASIFA Board any more, ASIFA Board of Directors
consists of the representatives of all national groups.

ASIFA inaugurated the International Animation Day.
October 28 was proclaimed as International Animation Day, commemorating
the first public performance of Emile Reynaud's Theatre Optique at the Grevin
Museum in Paris in 1892.

ASIFA: PAST,
PRESENT,
FUTURE...

I had been a member of ASIFA for many years, but somewhere along the way - maybe 10 years ago - I let my membership lapse. It wasn't a conscious decision; I just forgot to renew it. The years slipped by until I was asked to contribute to a discussion of ASIFA's future. Since then, I've been thinking about ASIFA and asking myself why I joined in the first place, why I lost my connection to the organization, and why I might want to renew my membership again.

Looking Forward

Workshop in SAF Cakovec
2003 with Fernando
Galrito (Portugal).

I first joined ASIFA in the mid-1980's, just after I completed my MFA in Experimental Animation at California Institute of the Arts. I had recently moved from Los Angeles to Providence to work at the Rhode Island School of Design. I set up a studio at home so that I could continue making personal animated films. I joined ASIFA then as part of my transition from student to independent filmmaking.

At that time, most of us made animation on film, with Oxberries, rewinds, splicing blocks, colour negative, reel to reel recorders, and laboratories. We saw films in theatres, festivals, and videotape compilations. Films made in the Communist countries were not generally available.

Workshop at SAF Cakovec 2008 with
Ekaterina Mikhaylova (Russia).

We had to go to festivals to see them, or somehow acquire a bootleg copy. Connecting with other filmmakers was difficult. Without the internet, festivals were our primary networking tools.

So festivals were extremely important, and they were one of the main reasons I joined ASIFA. I knew that if ASIFA endorsed a festival, it was more likely to be a positive experience, and the festivals gave some nice perks for members. I often paid a lower entry fee, and I sometimes got a discount on festival passes. At major festivals, I could attend ASIFA meetings, ASIFA screenings, and ASIFA parties. This was a great way to connect with other filmmakers from around the country and around the world - especially people from the Soviet bloc. ASIFA was like an international, apolitical club.

Antran Manoogian, Bill Dennis,
and Nelson Shin at Xiamen Animation Festival,
China 2009.

one of the original pinscreens made by Alexandre Alexeieff Board.

Since then, ASIFA's role as a bridge between Eastern bloc animators and their counterparts in the West has evaporated, advances in digital technology have transformed the way we make and view animation, and the internet has transformed the way we communicate. There are many more festivals, and ASIFA is less present and less significant in them. In addition, there are all sorts of on-line screening sites, blogs, and virtual festivals that have little in common with traditional festivals.

With the liberation from film and videotape, animation has even left the traditional screen. People freely incorporate animation into theatre, dance, opera, performance art, and installation art. ASIFA became less relevant to me. Membership no longer provided the same benefits for festival participation, and I mostly connect with other filmmakers through the internet and e-mail.

Perhaps the problem is that where I live, we have no ASIFA chapter. It would be great to have a local chapter that offered regular meetings, an opportunity for members to

Shipu of Bangladesh, Corinne Desroches, and Deanna Morse in Hiroshima 2008.

From left: William Dennis (Bill Dennis), Prashant Buyyala, Jeff Kleiser, Shelley Page, Vaibhav Kumaresh & Sohail at the ASIFA-India International Animation Day Celebration 2010.

screen personal work, screenings and talks by guest artists, technical workshops, a cultural calendar, a job board, and a message board for posting news, opinions, and information about local animation-related topics. I imagine my local ASIFA group including makers of games, interactive art, performance, and installation art. I wonder if there would there be a way for my local chapter to build its own archives that might eventually become part of a wider network of ASIFA archives. Whatever shape it took, the greatest value of a local chapter would be the opportunity to meet other animators, face to face.

Other than starting up more local chapters, some other thoughts occur to me. I live in an area with a number of film schools, and I wonder if there is a way to involve animation students more directly with ASIFA.

Te Wei and Georges Schweigebel.

Maybe ASIFA could charge lower membership fees for students. Students could use ASIFA to meet with professionals, line up internships, and get to know other students, after graduation, many of them will be colleagues. I also wonder if a local chapter could get local festivals involved with ASIFA. For example, in exchange for ASIFA sponsorship and advertising, perhaps a festival could offer local members entry fee or ticket discounts. An entirely new endeavour for ASIFA might be to sponsor an animation residency/arts centre where animation artists could come for short stays to work on projects, see public screenings and performances, view artwork, attend lectures, and spend time together.

Fundamentally, I see ASIFA as an umbrella community of animation-makers based on their love of the art form,

ASIFA Workshop Group (AWG) Meeting in Annecy 1997

rather than on any particular commercial, educational, or artistic special interest. This is a wonderful time for animators, when the practice of animation is expanding in all sorts of new creative directions. More than ever before, people involved in making animation have much to learn from each other. An organization which exposes animators to a wide variety of creative approaches can truly help to challenge, invigorate and advance our art form. To keep ASIFA relevant, I would like to see it make the umbrella bigger to include more types of animation makers, and I would like to see it provide more concrete membership benefits. I don't know what the future of ASIFA will look like, but it has the potential to grow and to thrive.

By the way, I renewed my international ASIFA membership while writing this article.

Steve Subotnik

Nicole Salomon and Pierre Azuelos at ASIFA Booth in Annecy 1997

Steve Subotnik is an independent animator and teacher living in Providence, RI.

JOHN HALAS

By Viven Halas

From a meeting in Annecy in 1961. In those days the meetings were small. From left to right: Raymond Maillet, Ivanov-Vano, John Halas, Joy Batchelor, Pierre Barbin and Paul Grimault. My father, always keen to keep good diplomatic relations between nations, told me that Ivanov-Vano the head of Soviet Animated Film Studios was most unhappy because they were offered only morning tea. This did not fit with Soviet expectations of vodka. After some searching a bottle of Whiskey was found and an international incident avoided.

John Halas was deeply involved in ASIFA, he first acted as treasurer, then as director general and vice president until he was elected president in 1976, a position he held until he finally retired in 1985. He was concerned with every aspect of animation and believed, as did my mother Joy Batchelor, that animation was the best form of artistic expression, as it brought all the elements of drawing, painting, music and movement together. In fact you might say that he hoped to save the world through animation and that ASIFA was an important part of that hope.

Reading through his President's letters it is clear that the same concerns that we have today were tackled: content, markets, distribution, technology and from his President's letter No11 from 1979:

Vivien Halas.

"Animation is not a religion neither is it a political movement in any sense. It remains a true contemporary art form which has been unrecognized for what it can achieve...... We consider animation as a universal expression which is capable of immense contribution if given a chance."

John would have been pleased to see how, in it's 50th year, ASIFA has grown and how there are now animation workshops all over the world. He would have been especially gratified to experience the new technology that he always championed and predicted.

According to Clare Kitson, Edward Nazarov, Jimmy Murakami and Nicole Salomon my father, John Halas, always managed to take no notice of any squabbles or heated arguments between the ASIFA members. He calmly proceed as if all was well and even when the Cold War got heated he managed to bring together a disparate group of egos and somehow keep his mind on what he considered to be the important issues, animation not politics. Bill Littlejohn, John Halas, Feodor Khitruk at Hiroshima 1987.

INTERNATIONAL ANIMATED FILM ASSOCIATION CONFERENCE

Ivan Ivanov-Vano, Head of Soviet Animated Film Studios, John Terry, Managing Director of the National Film Finance Corporation, and John Halas, Director General of the International Animated Film Association, and Creative Director of Halas & Batchelor, at a lunch given by Halas & Batchelor at the Dorchester Hotel in honour of the overseas delegates.

(Left to right) Max Massimino Garnier, Italy, Gyula Macskassy, Hungary, Joachim Kreck, W. Germany, Mrs. Garnier, Italy, Katja Georgi, E. Germany, John Terry, Gunar Karlssen, Sweden, Mrs. Fleet, U.S.A., Mr. Steward, Films Officer for Mullard Ltd., and Sandy Fleet, U.S.A., at the Dorchester.

This week for the first time the International Animated Film Association held a conference in Great Britain, hosted by its Director General, John Halas.

31 representatives from 15 nations attended, to discuss matters affecting the future of animated film. The topics under discussion included better marketing facilities for entertainment and TV cartoons, better use of animated in advertising and the expanding opportunities in educational films. New tchniques and co-production were also on the agenda.

The congress, which lasted for nine days, included a visit to Pinewood Studios, to the leading animation studios in London, a screening of the work of the British Animation Group, a symposium on animation at the National Film Theatre and a gala performance of the best animation of 1969 at the Baker Street Classic Cinema.

ASIFA at the International Animation Festival in Rimini, Italy, 1962 – at the table: John Halas (left), Robert Cannon (holding a glass), Norman McLaren (left of unknown man with face turned from camera), Joy Bachelor; Borivoj(Bordo) Dovnikovic is standing in the background.

The Beginning of ASIFA

When we study the birth of ASIFA, and the reasons why this organization was created, we can see how necessary it was in this post war period.

As soon as the second world war ended, there were some attempts to share information and activities about making different kinds of cinema, amongst which was the animated film. Some directors began to join forces by creating festivals, publishing magazines and building connections beyond borders. Some cinematheques in the world were already proposing special screenings of animated films.

In the mid 50's, the idea of promoting a different kind of cinema and having a better communication between artists whatever their origin was in the air.

A little bit of history

From the 25th April to the 1st May 1956, during the IX° Cannes festival, the first 'Journées Internationales du Cinéma d'Animation', JICA, was held for the first time. An exhibition about animated film was also organized at the Miramar hotel. John Halas & Joy Batchelor, Alexandre Alexeieff & Claire Parker, Paul Grimault, Henri Gruel, Jean Image, Jean Jabely, Gilbert Métral, Wlodimierz Haupe, Eduard Hofman, Jiri Trnka, Karel Zeman, Stephen Bosustow, John Hubley, Lev Atamanov and Ivan Ivanov-Vano were present. A dream committee! This event would later become the Annecy Festival.

Cannes 1956 - clockwise: unidentified, unidentified, Ivanov-Vano, Karel Zeman, Jiri Trnka, unidentified, Paul Grimault, Alexandre Alexeieff, Claire Parker, Jean Jabely, André Martin, Pierre Barbin, and Henri Gruel.

Annecy Animation Festival, 1977.

In 1958, a second session of this JICA was organized, again in Cannes. It was the success of these first professional meetings that gave these artists the idea of creating an association that could help them to keep in contact and share information.

In the end, an animated film director's international congress was organized between the 8th and 10th of June, 1960, during the first Annecy festival, alongside this first competitive formula. The idea was to inform interested parties about the specific aesthetic, technique and economics of animation in every country. A filmmaker from every represented country was allowed to make a maximum 30 minutes long speech. Eleven members from the 18 countries represented at the festival indicated their desire to see an international organization created.

Eventually, through four work sessions, the idea emerged for an international association linked to national or even regional groups. All were conscious of the necessity to take the time to prepare everything carefully. And eventually, in the last issue of the festival newspaper, the name CICA (Centre International du Cinéma d'Animation) appeared for the very first time. An international commission was created with two main goals: one was to study possible links between every professional in the world, and the second was to help with the promotion and understanding of animated film. In order to succeed, they still needed time: more discussions would be necessary and actually it took a few years before the ASIFA would emerge.

This first executive committee would meet again in Bergamo (Italy, Sept. 1960), in Tours (France, Dec. 1960), in Belgrade (Yugoslavia, May 1961) and later in Prague (Czechoslovakia, Jan. 1962). The purpose of all these meetings was to create the Articles of the Association; in the meantime, the Commission took on the role of the future Board. The name 'ASIFA' was finally chosen (the first bulletin with this name was published in May 1961). A last congress was held during the Annecy Festival on 29th and 30th of June 1962 for a final approval.

With the financial help of the French government, its secretariat was located in Paris, and the publication of a quarterly bulletin in three languages was ensured. During the Spring of 1963, the Association became active.

As soon as ASIFA was born, 100 filmmakers asked to join the Association. Many more would join during the next decades.

Jury deliberations for Annecy Animation Festival 1963. From left: Boris Kolar, Paul Grimault, George Dunning (jury president), Nicole Salomon, Chuck Jones, Emanuelle Sezzati.

The goals of ASIFA:

Communication between professionals:

We have to remember the political situation at the time, with a world split into two parts. That's why Article 2 of the statutes insisted upon the idea «to establish worldwide communication between all who are professionally concerned with animation». In other words, art is international and artists should not have to be concerned with international borders. We can see traces of this concern when we read the original pages for the preparation of the Tours congress of 1960. The document was completed with handwritten annotations, adding words such as 'international friendship', 'pacific', 'free circulation of films', and additionally the name of UNESCO (United Nations Education, Scientific and Cultural Organization) is clearly designated.

This crucial point at a time when the internet didn't exist, telephone calls were very expensive, and the post was unreliable, reveals a true desire to share. This was especially true because the Zagreb school had already set a good example, which since it began had been largely inspired by American UPA. And because all the artists were for the most part out of the mainstream, they all understood the necessity of joining forces to build an animation community that was not based on Disney standards.

ASIFA Booth at Annecy Animation Festival 1997. From left: Eduard Nazarov, unidentified, Nicole Salomon, Vesna Dovnikovic, Pierre Azuelos.

Another quite important point was that animation schools didn't yet exist, and films were made with very different and original techniques that were sometimes kept secret. Being able to talk about personal techniques was considered, even by professionals, an absolute necessity.

These points are, in my opinion, very important and should constitute a basis for a new definition of today's ASIFA's goals, as communication is now much easier than before. In other words, today's ASIFA can't have the same purpose as yesterday's ASIFA.

Also, as the opportunities to watch films were rare at that time, Pierre Barbin in Prague (in 1962), suggested that every important studio, or even every group of directors, send 5 recent films in 35mm or 16mm to the ASIFA, which would be in charge of their dispersal to other groups. The idea was for the professionals to exchange their films to facilitate a better knowledge of their respective productions.

First Post-graduate students of the Iranian Animation School and fresh ASIFA members at home meeting in 1977..

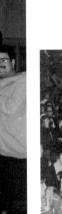

Information destined for the audience:

At the beginning of the 60's, animation was still ignored or apart from the main cinema. The general audience had very little idea of the non-Disneyesque production, particularly if we consider that personal short films were only screened for a few specialists. So, again in Article 2 of ASIFA's

Audience at Varna 1979.

statutes, we read «to inform government organizations and the public of the importance of animation Cinema in order to promote a more enlightened appreciation of this art form.» Very quickly after the creation of the Association, John Halas strongly requested the possibility of being able to screen foreign films through festivals and other outlets and an easier circulation of the prints beyond borders. This desire to have films travelling everywhere was, however, subject to the availability of prints (very expensive at this time). Nevertheless, information screenings were quickly proposed and accomplished: in 1963, a special screening of French productions was held in London, organized by John Halas on the 21st November. This was followed by an English production screening in Paris a week later on the 30th.

Through a definition of animation:

The creation of ASIFA also presented a great opportunity for the filmmakers to define what animation really is. For them, it represented a way to delimit their common art; a kind of 'technical manifesto' so a draft of Article 5 of the statutes was moved into the preamble of the statutes. At first, a definition of animation mentioning "frame-by-frame" was put on paper, but this seemed too limited for some directors who, referring to Arcady, Pojar and McLaren's works, preferred to clarify and expand the original definition. The frame by frame process was kept, but a very interesting and poetic idea was added 'In an Animation Film, events take place for the first time on the screen'.

Thus we see that it was the creation of movement from scratch that was pushed to the forefront. A definition was not absolutely necessary, as every director and technician knew what animation was about. Beyond the desire to communicate about this art, it's a kind of family name they gave to themselves, a definition that specified their passion through a certain way of thinking and making film. This anecdote reveals to us how important it was for these pioneers to express their love for their art.

I would like to end with these words from Ion Popesco-Gopo writing about ASIFA on the first publication (May 1961, N°1): «It is said that all ships need a compass to help them steer a right course, know the route of other ships, and not to collide. This compass is directed by a magnetic point. »

This is ASIFA, the magnetic point intends to give direction to and guide the great venture which is the art of animation, and every one who is working in it.

Olivier Cotte

Olivier Cotte is a Paris based animation historian author of numerous books, a director, and a comic book scriptwriter.

Above: Ghylaine and Frederic Back
at Studio Lotus (Sayoko's studio)
Right: at Yuri Norstein's studio:
Rene Laloux, Nicole Salomon,
Yuri Norstein, Sayoko Kinoshita,
Borivoj Dovnikovic, Jiri Kubicek

ASIFA in the Present Time

In the summer of 1992 I was invited to the International Animated Film Festival in Hiroshima. My student film Bunt (Colorful) had been accepted for the competition program. The ten day trip changed my life. I was fascinated by the atmosphere of this exceptional festival, where I became friends with other international artists and spent an inspiring and exceptionally entertaining time with them. During the legendary picnic on the famous shrine island of Miyajima I became involved with ASIFA because some friendly and open-minded ASIFA representatives heartily welcomed me. I was an "angry young man" who was frustrated about the fact that many animation festivals were

ASIFA Board meeting in Esphino 2009. From Left Front Row: unidentified, Genevieve Georgesco (Romania), Monique Renault (Belgium), Bruno Edero (Switzerland), Sayoko Kinoshita (Japan), Vesna Dovnikovic, Bordo Dovnikovic (Croatia), Deanna Morse (USA Central)
Back Row: unidentified, Abi Fejo (Portugal), Ed Desroches (USA Colorado), Thomas Renoldner (Austria), Brett Thompson (USA Atlanta), Juliette Crochu (France), Johnchill Lee (China).

too conservative in their choices for their international competition programs. I wanted to see more experimental animation at these events.

On the boat trip to the island I had a long conversation with Norwegian Board Member Gunnar Strom, who was General Secretary of ASIFA at that time. Contrary to my expectations Gunnar strongly supported my position and immediately proposed that I should become a member of the International Board. During the festival I also met David Ehrlich who later became a good friend along with Sayoko and Renzo Kinoshita. They all gave me the exceptional feeling of being very friendly and I felt accepted by the international animation community. Two years later I was elected as a member of the ASIFA Board and I continue to fulfill the position of official representative of ASIFA Austria today.

My story typically explains how the organizational structure of ASIFA was already in the process of transforming in the 1990s. In 1960 ASIFA's leadership had been what we might call the "crème de la crème" of international animation artists. The most famous names from different countries from around the world formed the original ASIFA Board. Later the qualification criteria softened and journalists, teachers and even, as in my case, students could also be accepted as a candidate for the ASIFA Board. Following this change in criteria for membership to the Board it was only a logical consequence to also put the general form of government of ASIFA in question. Originally ASIFA had been a relatively small group acting internationally, but in the meantime local ASIFA Chapters were being founded in countries around the world. In the beginning all Board Members knew each other personally but now the candidates to the International Board (who were still nominated by the existing Board Members) were not known to every local ASIFA Group member, and so the principle of direct democracy no longer functioned.

roshima 1992: at Hiroshima Castle, from left: arlos Arguello, Petra Freeman, Philip Hunt, Tim olt, Michele Cornoyer, Thomas Renoldner

After numerous preparatory discussions, the ASIFA Extraordinary General Assembly held on June 5, 2003 accepted my proposal that the future ASIFA Board should be comprised of a representative from each local ASIFA Group. ASIFA had entered the period of parliamentary democracy.

The benefits of the new system are obvious. Since 2003 a number of new ASIFA Groups have been founded and each local ASIFA member knows that he or she will have a representative on the ASIFA Board. The downsides are also too obvious. The increasing numbers of ASIFA Board Members makes communication more complicated and time-consuming. One possible solution to this problem was proposed in the 2003 New Structure Paper, when it was suggested to give more decision making power into the hands of the Executive Board. Surely the future ASIFA Board will solve the detail problems which are the consequence of a very positive development: the international growth of our organization.

Thomas Renolder

Thomas lectures on Animation at the Academy of Fine Arts and the Vienna Art School. He is also a musician, filmmaker, producer, teacher, and film historian.

Digital Painting Competition as part of the International Animation Day 2010 Celebration.

Zagreb 2002: with many international animation people brought on stage by Thomas Renoldner after taking over the ASIFA Presidency from Abi Feijo who could not continue at the moment.

Ed Desroches, Sayoko Kinoshita, Nicole Salomon.

Thomas Renoldner, Sayoko Kinoshita, and Renzo Kinoshita.

Annecy festival
Jimmy Teru Murakami
from USA (left) &
Manuel Otero from France.
Opposite Page bottom:

 # Into the Abyss...

As we move ahead into the coming years, we constantly question where we are going and what will happen. The future is always uncertain. What will happen to ASIFA as it heads into the unknown?

ASIFA's statutes state: "The Association is founded in the firm belief that the art of animation can be enriched and greatly developed through close international co-operation and the free exchange of ideas, experience and information among all who are concerned with the art of animation." As well as: "It should help to promote progress towards peace and mutual understanding between all people." In this vein, we should be aware that ASIFA will continue in its attempts to bring animators from all over the globe together in solidarity and to build lasting relationships.

As Sayoko Kinoshita of ASIFA-Japan mentions, "Especially, as we are now experiencing serious disaster in Japan, I feel that 'human relationship' and 'human contact' --- including meeting each other, exchanging ideas, cooperating [with] each other […], respecting and appreciating each other --- is very important to enhance our encouragement and positive spirit [in the] establishment [and] development [towards] creativity."

It seems pretty important that while ASIFA continues promoting the art of animation that it should also promote the involvement of its members and find new ways for them to interact and develop relationships. Sharing a common interest with a friend on the other side of the world will build bridges to a far off community and give you the ability to talk through ideas and work together with someone who may have a completely different perspective on life.

Vranje 2002:
Miki Simonovic,
Nikola Majdak,
Sayoko Kinoshita,
Vesna and Borivoj
Dovnikovic,
Pencho Kunchev.

Toronto 1984: Bill Littlejohn and Fedor Khitruk

ASIFA wants you to find that friend and form the bonds that build strong communities even in a global society.

Deanna Morse of ASIFA-USA Central says, "[ASIFA] is about building a community of like-minded individuals. You can see evidence of that, over the years - that we have used animation as a common interest to build friendships and relationships across borders, across the earth, across cultural difficulties and through political disagreements. Our common ground is animation. We use that meeting ground to make relationships and share our passion for animation with each other - over the internet, through fax, at festivals, in person. Building those relationships, and those friendships, based on our common love of animation: that is what ASIFA is about. That is why it started, why it persisted, and why it will continue. Through those relationships, we share friendship, respect, information, ideas, laughter. We are not competing, we are sharing. We build community - all these things are aligned with the ideas of spreading peace. Long live ASIFA!"

To that end, perhaps some of what you'll see in the new world is an ASIFA that is strengthening its Festival Partnerships. An ASIFA that is looking to form sister chapters which would allow a chapter in Serbia to form bonds with a chapter in USA. An ASIFA that is finding new ways to share culture and build awareness.

Joelle Haight, Andy Mason and Wynn Greene at Denver Starz Film Festival, 2010

Olivier Cotte (France), David Ehrlich (USA), Bordo Dovnikovic (Croatia).

Gary Schwartz, Deanna Morse, Corinne Desroches, Ed Desroches at Hiroshima 2008.

Of course, the friendships formed are what many members value most, but equally important is that ASIFA continue to serve as a body working to protect artist's rights. ASIFA may do this by reviewing how festivals treat artists, but also by looking at ways to protect the arts beyond the festivals. It is imperative that in a world where the internet has made many things free, from music downloads and video viewing, that ASIFA ensure the artists are not being robbed of their creations. ASIFA needs to figure out how to help its animators in the changing marketplace, in the changing economy.

These are ASIFA challenges in the next decades and as it hopes to remain around for the next 50 years!

Ed Desroches

Ed is a Vice President of ASIFA and President of ASIFA-Colorado. Aside from working in animation, digital editing, and web design and development Ed regularly holds children's animation workshops. He is an expert marksman and pacifist along with having a degree in eternal optimism.

The FESTIVALS

Animation LIVES in Festivals

Animation festivals are, for animators, like water is for fish: necessary for their survival. The channels for distribution of animation (e.g. DVD, internet) vary throughout the course of history, from one country to another, but festivals have retained an essential role for filmmakers.

Festivals are not only places to get a film screened—they are also important social and industrial spaces to meet colleagues, get feedback, and to explore distribution possibilities. Screenings, though, remain the centrepiece of a festival. Festival competitions and prizes can provide prize money to the filmmakers, help them solicit funding for their next projects, and attract the attention of buyers, recruiters, producers and other festivals.

KROK Animation Festival 2007.
Animator's Picnic.

The number of film festivals exploded in the 1990s. The reasons are many: technological advancements made the film production process faster and cheaper; new, compact formats made the distribution process more affordable. The relatively lost cost of creating DVDs—as opposed to 35mm film prints—enabled animators to submit their work to more festivals.

In 1996, the European Union estimated that there were more than 600 film festivals in the 15 EU member countries. The following year the estimate rose to 800 festivals. Today there are more than one thousand festivals in Europe alone.

Annecy Animation Festival at ASIFA Booth. 2007 ASIFA President, Sayoko Kinoshita and Secretary General, Vesna Dovnikovic.

Not all of these events are large, but, by the late 1990s, the European Audiovisual Observatory estimated that the number of spectators at film festivals in Europe would be in the range of 12.5 million. This figure is not insignificant compared with a commercial cinema audience.

In animation the growth has been very noticeable. In the late 1980s, the scene was dominated by the traditional festivals (i.e. Annecy, Zagreb, Ottawa, Hiroshima), but now the world map is full of animation festivals. This is the case especially in Europe, where animation festivals can also enjoy public financing, guaranteeing continuity and artistic freedom. Not every new festival is successful. Some, notably in the USA, have struggled to create successful, long-term events.

Despite the rise of new animation festivals, the big and well established festivals remain the most popular with both filmmakers and audiences. Animation festivals like Stuttgart, Annecy, Zagreb, Hiroshima, Ottawa and SICAF are well known, financed, organized and programmed. While their foundations are somewhat similar, each festival is unique in terms of its profile, programming and events.

Most major festivals have separate international competition selection committees that change annually. This method provides a festival with diverse perspectives and tastes, making for a well-rounded competition. There are also good examples of festivals where the competition is selected and programmed by a competent and innovative festival programmer.

There are also a growing number of well-organized and ambitious animation festivals around the globe, too many to mention here. The most positive development is the globalization of animation festivals. We now have several energetic festivals in Latin America and Asia (notably China) and even a new one in Africa.

Bordo Dovnikovic tries on a hat when visiting a hat factory as part of the Cinanima Animation Festival Outing, 2010.

To be a smaller festival does not necessarily mean that the event will be worse than a major one. On the contrary, some festivals with limited resources specialize in a specific genre or geographical area. Using this method, these festivals are often worth visiting because of their often excellent showcases of the films in their specialized area.

Competition among the festivals is hard: who will get best programs, important guests and fresh, interesting films in competitions? The multitude of animation festivals today make it very difficult to achieve these three goals.

While it is relatively easy to construct a festival with eager staff and volunteers, it is somewhat more challenging for organizers to maintain its existence on a long-term basis. Enthusiasm aside, a festival must have a solid financial and organizational structure in place. I have a semi-serious theory that the real essence of new film festivals is not visible until their third, fourth and fifth editions. By now, they should have already learned a lot of the practical side of organizing the event and how to run the business.

How can a filmmaker evaluate whether she should send her film to a specific festival or not? There is no clear yardstick to use, but by carefully reading the festival website, one can get some idea of what the event offers to filmmakers.

Goldfish Festival Outing 1996. From left: Borivoj (Bordo) Dovnikovic, Nicole Salomon, Jiri Kubicek, Otto Alder, Sayoko Kinoshita.

The cornerstone of a festival is usually—but not always—a competition. If there is no competition, it might be a event that wants to get films for free by calling itself a "festival". Also worth checking is whether an "international" competition is genuinely international. The previous competitions are often listed on a festival's web-page.

What about the prizes? It is not automatic that a big prize makes a good festival. Many festivals in small countries with minimal resources are sincere even though the prize money is small. But if there are good prizes, it shows that the sponsors do appreciate the festival.

Traditionally all festivals invite all directors of the competition films to the festival, offering accommodation and food vouchers. The level of hospitality speaks volumes about the festival's view of the filmmakers. Some festivals even go so far as to pay for the travel expenses of competition filmmakers.

Competition regulations should be read thoroughly. Does the festival return preview copies or keep them in their archive? What rights do they have for using the prints? Are the films screened elsewhere? Are the film prints, tapes or DVDs insured by the festival?

Any event can call itself a festival. Some are more or less rip-offs, trying to get films without giving anything to the filmmakers or producers. One of the worst cases

I encountered was at a small short film festival. By signing the festival's entry form, the entrant was giving away all distribution and publishing rights to the festival. When I contacted the festival they changed the rules. The moral of the story is: always read the rules before sending your film.

Strange authors' rights regulations can also appear in many competitions. Even the Commission of the European Union had a video competition that took very broad distribution rights of the films from the filmmaker. When approached, the Commission of these unfair competition rules replied that there is nothing wrong with them. The filmmaker gets fame, and isn't that what he wants? Well, filmmakers need to pay for their bread or rice, too, and for this reason they are selling distribution rights, not signing these away for free.

The main thing is, however, important to remember: film festivals are an animator's best friend. Festivals are worth visiting and supporting. Without festivals, there would be a huge void in the world of animation. Without festivals, we would all know much less about animation and have fewer colleagues as friends. Without festivals, many of us would be a fish on dry land.

Heikki Jokinen

Heikki is ASIFA Vice-President and serves as a liaison between ASIFA and festivals.

Bill Littlejohn,
Zarrinkelk Junior Farhang,
Faith Hubley and
Noureddin Zarrinkelk Senior
at Annecy Animation Festival 1995.

Festival 7-12 June   Mifa 9-11 June

Annecy 2010
International animation film festival

www.annecy.org

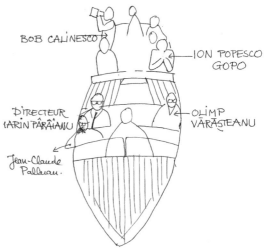

BOB CALINESCO

ION POPESCO GOPO

DIRECTEUR IARIN PÂRÂIANU

OLIMP VARASTEANU

Jean-Claude Palluau.

Realisateurs roumains :
- Ion Popesco GOPO
- Bob Calinesco
- Olimp Varasteanu
Directeur - Marin Pârâianu - ex
sécrétair Général ASIFA.

The Beginnings: ASIFA and Annecy Festival

To answer to numerous questions about the Annecy event and the birth of ASIFA, I suggest reading two documents: "1960-1985 Annecy Festival" and "ASIFA 30 Years". Although they are quite old, they have serious roots and they name the true pioneers of both events. No ridiculous declarations involving General de Gaulle being responsible for the birth of Annecy festival. I am not an historian but I have been an active witness since 1960. I would like to acknowledge the role of Pierre Barbin, the first director of Annecy festival and ASIFA Secretary General. I would like to acknowledge the dedication of the Annecy ciné-club voluntary members. And I also would like to emphasize the unlimited help that ASIFA gave to Annecy festival.

In 1982, when Annecy festival was rejuvenated (as I had been elected on the ASIFA board), I received tremendous help from ASIFA board colleagues. Therefore, Annecy festival got from ASIFA all contacts and links with the international world of artists. Thanks to ASIFA and its President John Halas, the festival could go on. ASIFA started the "Festival Boutique" in a small booth in the Bonlieu lobby, before it was shuffled to a lower level, as the festival created a bigger boutique. It was an ASIFA idea. It was also another idea of ASIFA to present an exhibition in the Annecy public library: a Russian works exhibition, Michel Ocelot exhibition, Alison de Vere exhibition...all tributes to artists we love.

At the old prisons of Annecy in 1965. From left: Maurice Blackburn, Evelyn Lambart, Norman Mc Laren, Grant Munro.

At a cafe during the Annecy Animation Festival 2010 - clockwise around the table from left Vesna Dovnikovic, Yung Shin, Johnchill Lee with his wife, Agnus Lee, Ji yeun Yi, Ed Desroches, and Nelson Shin,

It is also thanks to ASIFA that we could start our Annecy workshops (AAA or Atelier de Cinéma d'Animation d'Annecy) and get the participation of so many great artists in our activities for young people: Alexandre Alexeïeff and Claire Parker, Faith Hubley, Edward Nazarov, Bob Godfrey, Josko Marusic, Bratislav Pojar, Kihachiro Kawamoto, Alison de Vere, etc.

Being a native of Annecy, I want to thank ASIFA with all my heart for what has been given to Annecy by this international association.

A past mayor of Annecy once said: "A Annecy, un service n'est jamais pardonné (In Annecy, great favours are never forgiven)!" Let's hope that the orientation taken by Annecy festival will no longer illustrate this local bad reputation.

Nicole Salomon

Nicole is a long time Annecy resident and ASIFA member as well as ex-Secretary General of ASIFA.

Mamaia Film Festival

Following the genesis of ASIFA and the Annecy International Animation Festival in the 1960s, a new animation festival began in Romania.

Romanian animation has a long history that dates back to around 1927. In 1955, a department for animated films existed in the Bucharest Studios in Buftea (a small town near Bucharest). Several well-known animators, such as Ion Popescu Gopo, Matty Aslan, Bob Calinescu, and others, have worked at the studio.

In 1957, Ion Popescu Gopo's short animation, A Brief History, won the Palme d'Or and many other international prizes. Inspired by Popescu's success, Romanians began to embrace animation as a major art form. In 1965, the animation departments of the Bucharest film studios, became an independent animation studio, ANIMAFILM, with headquarters in Bucharest.

With this newfound appreciation of animation as an art form, the Mamaia festival was born in 1966. The Mamaia festival was held every two years, under the aegis of the National Cinema Centre, Filmmakers' Association of Romania and ASIFA. The heart and soul of the festival took the form of Ion Popescu Gopo and Marin Paraianu. The event's motto was "Imagination at the Service of Humanity".

As Pierre Barbin said in 1968, "Mamaiannecy is not a bicephalous monster escaped from Swift's tales, but a state of mind... Mamaia today, Annecy yesterday, but also Annecy tomorrow and Mamaia the day after tomorrow: thanks to them, the animation cinema may progress...."

AL TREILEA FESTIVAL INTERNAȚIONAL
AL FILMULUI DE ANIMAȚIE MAMAIA 70

LE TROISIEME FESTIVAL INTERNATIONAL
DU FILM D'ANIMATION MAMAIA 70

23 — 28 juin 1970

Norman McLaren's film images.

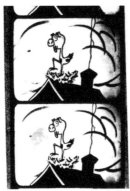

Quelques uns des personnages de Aurel Petresco («Les animaux bizzares»)

Hapléa, le héros de Marin Iorda,

The Mamaia festival took place in 1966, 1968 and 1970. The juries of these festivals included diverse personalities from the world of animation. Other big names entered the competition and vied for the top awards: the Golden (or Silver) Pelican.

Some of the most famous members of the jury or competition included: John Halas, Yoji Kuri, Raoul Servais, Donio Donev, Bruno Bozzetto, Paul Grimault, Ivan Ivanov-Vano, Dusan Vukotic, Feodor Khitruk, Ernest Ansorge, William Littlejohn and many others. We are proud that foreign and Romanian filmmakers won these prizes in Mamaia.

The ASIFA General Assembly was held during the third edition of the Mamaia festival in June 1970. During this time, ASIFA's regular newsletter, the ASIFA Bulletin (an essential means of connecting the international animation community) was also published in Romania, at the ANIMAFILM Studio.

After the festival's third edition, economic problems forced the Romanian state to cut subsidies and, unfortunately, this meant the end for these wonderful international animation meetings.

Despite the festival's demise, Mamaia lives on in the memories and hearts of animation people and Romanian ASIFA members.

Genevieve Georgesco

Genevieve is an animator and ASIFA Board Member.

Je nacquis sur la planète Terra, continent Europe, pays Roumanie, ville Bucarest, quartier Bellu, dans la maison paternelle, en 1923, 1-er mai. Comme tous les gosses de 4 ou 5 ans, je voulais devenir «médecin pour femmes». Je ne parvins à être que metteur en scène. Le microbe du cinéma c'est mon père qui me l'a passé, lui-même cinéaste. En 1939 j'ai fait un film de 16 mètres. J'étais, paraît-il, affreusement content de mes qualités artistiques. Ce fut à peine dans les ateliers de sculpture de l'Académie des Beaux Arts que j'appris à faire une main avec cinq doigts.

J'ai fait des dessins pour la presse, pour les maisons d'édition. J'ai commencé à faire des films dessinés et, bien entendu, j'ai appris comment on dessine une main à quatre doigts, telle que la portait Mickey Mouse. Un beau jour, j'ai reçu le grand prix à Cannes pour «Courte histoire», où le petit bonhomme dessiné par moi avait une main aux doigts en forme de balai.

Outre l'importance accordée à l'évolution des doigts de la main, j'ai aussi des préoccupations plus étendues. Mes admirateurs pour le film dessiné me reprochent d'avoir permis à mes interprètes d'employer des mains à cinq doigts.

Mon rêve d'avenir? Que les martiens voient mon film «Homo sapiens».

LE
II-EME
FESTI
VAL IN
TERNA
TIONAL
DU
CINE
MA
D'ANI
MATION
MAMAIA
'68

EDITION
SPECIALE
DE
LA REVUE
cinema

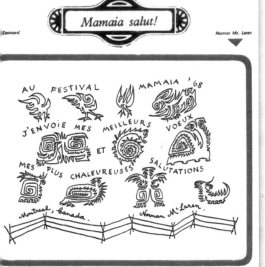

AU FESTIVAL MAMAIA '68
J'ENVOIE MES MEILLEURS VOEUX
ET
MES PLUS CHALEUREUSES SALUTATIONS
Montreal, Canada. Norman McLaren

Mamaia salut!

Zaninović   Norman Mc. Laren

Counter-clockwise from below:
Norman McLaren drawings for Mamaia,
Mamaiannecy article by Marin Pîrîianu
and Pierre Barbin, Catalog cover 1968,
Article about Ion Popesco Gopo.

Le festival d'animation au passé, au présent et au futur

MAMAIANNECY

Dans l'attente de l'important événement, à la veille de l'ouverture de la deuxième édition du Festival International du Film d'Animation, je suis gagné par une forte émotion.

Emotion d'autant plus grande qu'en notre qualité d'hôtes nous sommes préoccupés d'offrir à nos invités les meilleures conditions, pour ne pas démentir la chaleureuse et bien connue hospitalité roumaine, — et de continuer en même temps, les bonnes traditions de collaboration amicale, établies entre notre festival et celui d'Annecy.

Le développement extrêmement rapide et la multilatéralité des formes et méthodes enregistrées dernièrement dans la réalisation des films d'animation, l'intérêt suscité dans le monde artistique par ces oeuvres, attirent vers ce genre, des artistes de tous les domaines. Et le rythme de ce développement, impose la large et systématique confrontation, de plus en plus compétente, des réalisations des animateurs du monde entier.

En ce sens, nous désirons que le Festival de Mamaia '68, offre à tous les créateurs du 8-ème art, la possibilité de connaître les oeuvres de leurs collègues, de faire le bilan de leurs activités, de discuter sur les directions du développement ultérieur de l'animation, et d'établir des amitiés en vue d'une collaboration qui ne peut-être qu'utile à nous tous.

Le mot d'ordre sous lequel se déroule le Festival International du film d'animation, «l'imagination de l'homme au service de l'humanité», offre un cadre digne aux plus nobles et hautes tendances et idéaux de l'homme contemporain, dans le contexte de l'effort général du monde entier vers le progrès et la paix.

Dans l'espoir que le Festival de Mamaia contribuera à l'affermissement de la paix mondiale et au développement d'une animation dévouée à l'humanité, nous adressons à nos invités un chaleureux «Soyez les bien venus!» — sous le soleil éclatant de Mamaia.

Marin PÎRÎIANU

Comme dans la vie quotidienne, il est agréable de penser qu'on participera, au moins une fois l'an, à la fête d'un ami et l'on ne sait plus très bien, le jour venu, si c'est soi-même ou l'autre qui est le plus heureux! La joie de l'animation c'est la nôtre et sa fête, qu'elle se déroule à Mamaia ou à Annecy, est notre fête.

Mamaiannecy n'est pas un monstre bicéphale échappé des contes de Swift, c'est un état d'esprit, un choix, un culte que le monde entier rend à une multitude de petites divinités tendres ou ricanantes, voluptueuses ou caracolantes, revendicatrices ou narquoises, tour à tour rieuses, sévères, rêveuses, exacerbées, pitoyables ou terrifiantes mais toutes libres. C'est aussi un hommage rendu au beau et à l'ingéniosité, à l'intelligence et à la poésie. Mamaiannecy est le symbole barbare d'un art non domestique.

Mais Mamaia comme Annecy sont là pour enfermer dans le même écrin soyeux ces enthousiasmes aigus et par trop folâtres, pour discipliner — oh, pour quelques jours seulement — le talent capricieux venu se reposer nonchalamment au bord d'une mer après s'être diverti paresseusement au pied d'une montagne. L'entrechoquement redoutable de milliers d'images dynamitées une à une par des artificiers de génie ne saurait, en effet, s'accomoder de refuges moins agréables.

Mamaia aujourd'hui, Annecy hier, mais aussi Annecy demain et Mamaia après-demain: grâce à eux, le cinéma d'animation progresse, non comme un satellite fou ressassant sans cesse son même parcourt stupide, mais comme un jeune géant atteignant les plus hautes étoiles, les pieds rivés à ces deux grands ports.

Pierre BARBIN

Animafest: World Festival of Animated Film in Zagreb

Margit Antauer (Buba): laureat of ASIFA Prize 2007, Joanna Quinn: creator of ASIFA Prize, Sayoko Kinoshita: ASIFA President.

The World Festival of Animated Film in Zagreb is the second oldest festival in Europe completely dedicated to this unique art, promoting animated short films since 1972.

Neither war nor the drastic change of the political and economic system in the 1990s could upset its enduring, vital standing in the country's and city's cultural scenery. In the course of its forty-year-old history it has systematically been following world animation production through films

Zagreb Animation Festival 2002 - 30th Anniversary of World Festival of Animated Films in Zagreb.

Original Zagreb Festival Poster.

specially selected for its competition categories to point out new trends and present new filmmakers—never forgetting the educational component and value of historical, personal or national retrospectives—various screenings and lectures meant primarily for generations to come.

Built on the tradition of the Zagreb School of Animation (a movement defining the style of animation coming from this area), the festival is geared towards auteur film, still building a bridge between personal films and the increasing quality of studio productions.

The Festival was founded by the City of Zagreb and the production studio Zagreb Film and approved by the Executive Committee of ASIFA. The festival has hosted most renowned makers of animated film, gaining a large international reputation, always under the auspices of the International Association of Animators (aka ASIFA).

ZAGREB '88

Zagreb Animation Festival 1988.

ZAGREB '80

foto: S. knatlec

Zagreb Animation Festival 1980 picnic.

In 2005, Animafest introduced the program of animated feature film. Since then this biannual festival has turned into an annual event—each odd-numbered year is devoted to feature film and even-numbered one to the animated shorts.

Margit Buba Antauer

Margit, better known as Buba, is a long-term director of the World Festival of Animated Films in Zagreb, and 2007 ASIFA Prize Winner

Different views of an ASIFA Meeting at Zagreb Animation Festival 1988 - from left - Renzo Kinoshita, Yan Ding Xian, Howard Beckerman, Jerzy Kucia, Helene Tanguay, Jiri Kubicek, Antti Peranne, Priit Parn.

Zagreb downtown.

Ottawa International Animation Festival

Founded in 1975 by the Canadian Film Institute, and pulled together over a short nine months, the Ottawa International Animation Festival (OIAF) was born.

First held August 10 to 15, 1976, the OIAF created a gathering place for North American animation professionals and enthusiasts to ponder the craft and business of animation. It also provided their international colleagues with a unique opportunity to gain an appreciation for and access to the North American scene.

Many key players of Canadian animation banded together to help festival founders Bill Kuhns (who came up with the idea for a festival), Frederik Manter, Prescott J. Wright, Frank Taylor and the late Kelly O'Brien (who put it all together) organize North America's first event of its kind. ASIFA, ASIFA-Canada, the National Film Board of Canada, Radio Canada, CBC Television, and Cinémathèque Québécoise, among others, all had a hand in creating and building what is now North America's largest animation festival.

Canada's capital was a natural choice for an international animation festival. Home to animation innovator Norman McLaren, some of Canada's first private animation studios,

Ottawa Animation Festival 1990 picnic.

and the former headquarters of the National Film Board, Ottawa's animation community provided a nurturing atmosphere for the fledgling festival.

Main events of the first festival included screenings of films entered in and out of competition; a Forum for the Future seminar; a NFB art exhibition; Oskar Fischinger, Raoul Barré and Fleischer Brothers retrospectives; cut-collage and children's film compilations; hands-on animation workshops for young animators led by Co Hoedeman, Peter Foldes, and Caroline Leaf (imagine!); plus the world premiere of Italian animator Bruno Bozzetto's first feature film Allegro Non Troppo.

Norman McLaren served as the festival's first honorary president, a tribute that has been bestowed to legendary animators like Frédéric Back (1984), David Ehrlich (2002), and Co Hoedeman (2004), among others.

The Animator's Picnic, first held in 1976, became the social highlight of every festival, with animators—Oscar winners among them—fiercely competing for the best-carved pumpkin prize. Chez Ani, the nightly animators' café, founded by Co Hoedeman at the second festival in 1978, continues to provide festival participants with a place to unwind, meet with friends old and new, and broker the occasional deal.

Below: Prescott Wright at Ottawa Animation Festival 1978.
Right: Animators' Picnics

Left: Ottawa Aniboutique.
Right: John Canemaker and
Richard Williams.

Since the beginning, the OIAF has put out a call for entries for films to compete for festival prizes, including the prestigious Grand Prize, the festival's highest honour. Given the growing number of entries received over the years, the popularity and need for the festival has never been in doubt. Beginning with just over 400 films (over a two-year period) at the 1976 festival, the OIAF now receives upwards of 2100 submissions annually.

Categories continue to evolve in order to reflect the ever-changing nature of animation. In recent years, the festival has shifted its award category focus from celebrating the art of animation to recognizing the artistry behind both independent and commercial work. Animated features were added to the awards competition during OIAF 2002. The commissioned category was expanded to include animated adult and children television work for OIAF 2004.

Founded at the dawn of computer animation, the festival continues to display the latest in animation technology, while still celebrating the variety and talent behind so-called traditional animation. From the first computer-generated animation workshop led by National Research Council scientist Nestor Burtnyk in 1976 to the expansion of the New Media category from one umbrella to four sub-categories in 2004, the festival remains on the cusp of animation's cutting-edge.

To further meet industry needs, the OIAF organized its first-ever Television Animation Conference (TAC) in 2002, a chance for Canadian and international animation

Ottawa 2004 awards. Chris Landreth and Ryan Larkin on our stage accepting the Grand Prize award for "Ryan", to Chris' left is Mo Willems and to the right of Ryan are Signe Baumane and Gary Baseman.

producers, broadcasters, and buyers to network, discuss industry issues, and do business.

The OIAF went annual in 1997 with the establishment of the Ottawa International Student Animation Festival (SAFO). Held in alternate years to the larger OIAF, SAFO was the animation festival created to provide a venue solely for student and emerging animators to draw extra attention to their work. Children, high school, undergraduate, graduate and first-time filmmakers were provided with a distinct venue to show their films, discuss issues, and meet other young filmmakers.

When the OIAF moved from a biennial to an annual festival in 2005, the student categories become a part of the main festival. The OIAF is committed to ensuring the animation profession benefits from exposure to outstanding creativity and originality of emerging work, and young animators gain access to the movers and shakers of their chosen profession.

Overcoming an office fire in 1999, a move to Toronto in 1984, then Hamilton in 1986, and incessant government funding cuts, the Ottawa International Animation Festival has proven its resiliency and maintained its relevance for over three decades. Always popular, hundreds of guests traverse oceans and borders to attend the event.

Chris Robinson and Kelly Neall

Chris and Kelly are the Directors of the Ottawa International Animation Festival.

CINANIMA: The International Animated Film Festival of Espinho

Since 1977, CINANIMA has been held in Espinho, Portugal, a town which belongs to the metropolitan Area of Oporto and which is situated on the north coast of the country.

The festival has been held every single year since its foundation, so, it is now the oldest cinema festival in Portugal and one of the oldest animated film festivals in Europe.

It was established by Nascente—Cooperativa de Acção Cultural, CRL, and it has been co-organized by the Espinho Municipality for more than twenty years. The competition is divided into two different sections: an international

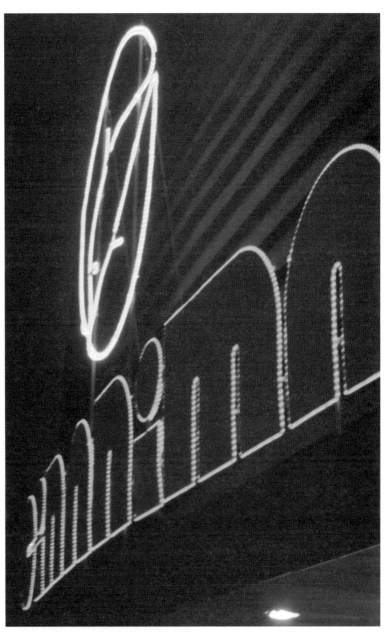

Neon sign of CINANIMA

Nearby Beach of CINANIMA

section for short, medium length films and features and a national section, with two awards. Besides this competitive program, the festival also programs non-competitive sessions to show retrospectives, special screenings and special sessions for children and young people. The festival has always invested in an educational area through the organization of workshops.

Sayoko Kinoshita and Antonio Gaio at Cinanima 1997.

Cinanima Audience.

CINANIMA is one of the partner festivals of Cartoon d'Or—the pan-European prize for the best animated short film. The Cartoon d'Or is organized with the support of MEDIA, the support program for the European audiovisual industry.

The awarded film at CINANIMA is also pre-selected for the Academy Awards in Hollywood for Best Animated Short.

The most significant animated films of the last 25 years have been screened in this festival, especially in its competitive sessions. This is what the organizing committee expects to continue for many years to come.

Antonio Gaio

Antonio is director of CINANIMA, The International Animated Film Festival of Espinho, Portugal, that celebrates its 35th edition this year, became its director 31 years ago, intensely working for the promotion of the art of animation. However, since a very early age, António Gaio has been involved in the promotion of culture and sports in Espinho and he is recognised as one of the most important personalities of this city.

ASIFA Board Meeting at Cinanima 2009

A Short History of Varna Festival

In October 1979 in the beautiful Bulgarian town Varna, situated along the coast of the Black Sea, the First World Animated Film Festival "Varna '79" took place. At the opening ceremony John Halas, the ASIFA President, said: "For many years nothing dramatic has ever occurred in any other art form outside of animation. Animation is the only free art which originated in our century. Animation has the greatest future of all".

At that time it seemed that Varna Festival would have a great future too. The following five biannual editions classified Varna as one of the important animated film festivals in the world, organized under the patronage of ASIFA together with the Annecy, Zagreb, Ottawa and Hiroshima festivals.

During the years Varna welcomed many famous animated filmmakers including Jan Lenica, Raoul Servais, Bretislav Pojar, Emanuele Luzzati, Paul Driessen, Yoji Kuri, Jean-Francois Lagionie, Yuri Norstein, and many others. Among the prize winners were such great films as Allegro non Troppo by Bruno Bozzeto, Interview by Caroline Leaf and Veronica Soul, Everything-Nothing by Frederic Back,

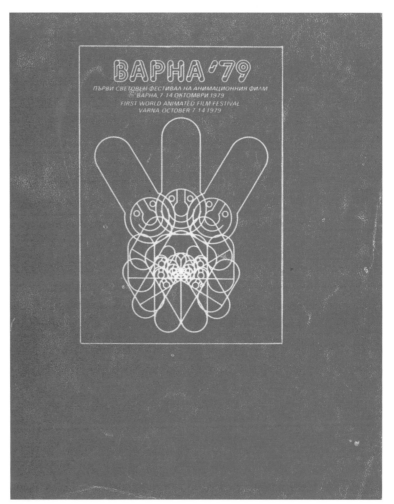

Varna Poster.

Varna 1981

From above, clockwise: John
Halas at Varna 1981.
Paul Driessen and Caroline Leaf;
Paul Dopff, Ernest Ansorge, and
Daniel Szczechura; Varna 1979 signs;
Jerzy Kucia receiving Grand Prix
at Varna 1987; Fedor Khitruk and
Renzo Kinoshita.

Fedor Khitruk

House of Flames by Kihachiro Kawamoto, The Vanished World of Gloves by Jiri Barta, and The Cow by Alexander Petrov.

Unfortunately after the political and economic changes in Bulgaria in 1989, the Varna Festival interrupted its existence for a long period of time. Regardless, the Varna Festival will remain as the greatest animation film festival ever organized behind the Iron Curtain, providing many animators from Soviet bloc countries a rare opportunity to view the depth and wonder of this unusual and magnificent art of moving drawings.

Since the autumn of 2010, there is an association in Sofia whose goal is to restore the Varna Festival. The seventh edition should be ready by September 2011. In this way, a bridge will be built between the glorious tradition of the past and the promising future.

Pencho Kunchev

Pencho is President of ASIFA Bulgaria and previous ASIFA Vice President.

From left: unidentified, Peter Szoboszlay, Renzo Kinoshita, Raoul Servais, and Stoyan Dukov at Varna 1979.

ПЪРВИ СВЕТОВЕН ФЕСТИВАЛ НА АНИМАЦИОННИЯ ФИЛМ ВАРНА 7 14 ОКТОМВРИ 1979

ПЕРВЫЙ МИРОВОЙ ФЕСТИВАЛЬ МУЛЬТИПЛИКАЦИОННЫХ ФИЛЬМОВ ВАРНА 7 14 ОКТЯБРЯ 1979

FIRST WORLD ANIMATED FILM FESTIVAL VARNA, OCTOBER 7-14 1979

PREMIER FESTIVAL MONDIAL DU FILM D'ANIMATION VARNA, 7-14 OCTOBRE 1979

Hiroshima:
International Animation
Festival in Japan

Shotaro Tanabe, Renzo
Kinoshita and Charles
Samu at Lappy Party
during Hiroshima 1985.

For twelve long years, since 1972, Renzo and Sayoko
Kinoshita were making every effort to realize an international animation festival in Japan. Then, their independent
animation short Pica Don (1978) moved the history. This
ten-minute documentary animation depicting the tragedy
of the atomic bomb showed the effectiveness of animation
media, and Takeshi Araki, mayor of Hiroshima at the time,
who had great foresight toward the possibility of animation
art, submitted the agenda of founding an animation festival.

On April 12, 1984, the Hiroshima City Council officially decided to establish the International Animation Festival in Japan—HIROSHIMA '85—as an event commemorating the 40th anniversary of the atomic bombing. This decision was immediately sent to ASIFA President John Halas, who kindly promised to send a letter in support of the festival.

In June 1984, during the ASIFA Board Meeting in Zagreb, ASIFA unanimously decided to patronize the HIROSHIMA Festival. Thus, from August 18 to 23, 1985, the First International Animation Festival in Japan—HIROSHIMA '85—was held as the only ASIFA Patronized festival in Asia, welcoming Paul Grimault, one of the founders of ASIFA, as the Honorary President, and co-organized by Hiroshima City and ASIFA-Japan.

As the first festival was held very successfully, a very difficult case occurred in 1986—that another animation organization tried to take over the festival while we were

Thomas Renoldner, Nikola Majdek, and Georges Schwizgebel - then below: Peter Lord, Eduard Nazarov, and Thomas Renoldner on the Hiroshima Hotel Floor in 1994.

preparing the second edition, HIROSHIMA '87. The ASIFA Board asked the representative of the HIROSHIMA Festival to attend the Board Meeting held in Canada during the Hamilton Festival (the 1986 site of the Ottawa Festival, held September 29-October 4) and to explain the situation. The Board proposed that ASIFA would withdraw patronizing the HIROSHIMA Festival—however, they decided to continue the patronage after Renzo Kinoshita promised to organize the festival properly. During HIROSHIMA '87, the ASIFA Honorary President John Halas and General Secretary Nicole Salomon clarified the problem at a meeting with ASIFA-Japan members as well as other Japanese animation people, and, in order to solve the problem, they firmly expressed that ASIFA would support HIROSHIMA Festival only on the condition that the festival is organized by ASIFA-Japan.

HIROSHIMA Festival continues pursuing perpetual world peace through cross-cultural exchange by promoting the animation art culture. Under the spirit of ASIFA and Hiroshima, this festival has long been organized by the leadership of Sayoko Kinoshita, treating artists and film-makers with utmost respect.

Text by ASIFA-Japan

Nelson Shin, Ed Desroches, Sayoko Kinoshita, Wiola Sowa, Anastasia Dimitra, Johnchill Lee, Noureddin ZarrinKelk, and Deanna Morse (ASIFA Board Members) during Hiroshima 2010.

Dangerous Crow in
Hiroshima Festival.

Gerrit van Dijk,
Bill Littlejohn, John Halas
at a Press Conference
during Hiroshima 1985.

Sayoko Kinoshita.

Clockwise from left: Sayoko Kinoshita and Raoul Servais,
Nicole Salomon, Makiko Nagao , Nelson Shin, and Noureddin
ZarrinKelk in 2010 Hiroshima, at ASIFA evening.

SAYOKO KINOSHITA

Interview By Anastasia Dimitra

Why are you a member of ASIFA?

SK- Because I liked and respect very much the founders of ASIFA.

Do you have the impression that nowadays ASIFA promotes the animators' benefits?

The time that we were only showing films has passed, nowadays, we have to pay back to the artists the rights of their work, in this sense. I am confident that if the IAD (International Animation Day) project could manage to pay back the rights, it will be a wonderful project that will promote the ideas of ASIFA.

What connected ASIFA members?

ASIFA-Japan's 62 members are very connected because they have common targets, their strongest bond is their love for animation. So, they enter into the association to offer what they can, without benefits. They are volunteers and they try hard to collect money for the ASIFA international. But international ASIFA is different, it's more difficult for all members to be connected, because of cultural and geographical differences.

What do you think is the future of our Association?

First of all, to carry on the spirit of the founders. It's not that I am living in the past, but I like to follow the ideas of our founders. The animation media has become divided in categories today (e.g. animation for the museum installations, for entertainment, video games, virtual reality performances) so ASIFA has to meet those changes of animation art.

Today, all these categories are mixed and perhaps we must divide. ASIFA should establish financially independent groups. I think that AWG (ASIFA Workshop Groups) is a successful example of an ASIFA independent group that can copy ASIFA for the above mentioned categories to be more independent and experimental.

Sayoko Kinoshita during SICAF 2005.

SICAF:
Seoul International Cartoon
and Animation Festival

Founded in 1995, SICAF (Seoul International Cartoon and Animation Festival) is an annual cartoon and animation event held in August.

The birth of SICAF was very timely in Korea. A plan to promote the Korean cultural industry was devised by the government in order to create a foundation for the animation sector and to give hope to young Koreans who desired to become animators. The government then decided to create the SICAF festival.

Initially, SICAF received mainly private funds from animation production studios, toy enterprises and cable network stations. Other major supporters were the Ministry of Culture and Sports, the Korea Cartoonists Association and Korea Animation Producers Association.

In the past, parents frowned upon their children's desires to become cartoonists or animators. This attitude prevented young Koreans from following their passions. The emergence of SICAF revealed to Korean parents that animation and cartooning could be a profitable and respectable career choice.

SICAF Characters

A section of SICAF Festival

Soon, the popularity of cartoons and animation exploded throughout Korea. As a result, like bamboo shoots sprouting after the rain, many animation departments were established in hundreds of colleges and universities. Animation became so popular that a high school devoted to animation was eventually created.

In the beginning of 1995, I took charge collecting films to screen at our festival. Some of the delegates and I went to the Annecy festival in France. There, we met Michel Ocelot, the president of ASIFA at the time, Nicole Solomon, the secretary-general, and treasurer, Pierre Azuelos.

We introduced SICAF and requested their assistance in soliciting films for our festival. They were probably puzzled at our request. Later we received 33 original European creative films and screened them in SICAF. For the cartoon section of the festival, we invited cartoons that had been exhibited permanently at Angulem in central France and made them available to exhibit at SICAF. This gave us the opportunity to introduce Koreans to various forms of animation.

from left: Luca Raffaelli,
Jiyoon Yang, Nelson Shin,
Igor Prassel, Jiyeun Yi,
Zhang Fu Gui.

In the past 15 years, the basic objective of the government has been "promoting cultural exports through the nurturing of cartoons and animation" but, as administrations have changed several times during this period, the government's initiative has waned. However, the education and support activities of SICAF have developed and expanded each year through university lectures and other creative activities of considerate directors.

In 2005, the Board of Directors of ASIFA made a very significant decision at the request of SICAF. Having developed the festival according to international rules, we asked, and received, formal certification from ASIFA.

Today, SICAF has become one of ASIFA's official partner festivals and has established itself as one of the major international animation festivals along with Annecy, Hiroshima, Zagreb and Ottawa.

Nelson Shin

Nelson is an animation producer, animator, professor, CEO of AKOM studio, editor-in-chief of ANIMATOON and President of ASIFA.

ASIFA members in SICAF 2005.

Performance Actor
at Xiamen Animation
Festival 2009.

What Makes a Good Festival?

There is a difference between a film festival and a film screening. A festival is not an occasional special program in a local art cinema—it is an event that requires significant planning, work, and passion to make it happen.

What does a festival need to be a good event? To answer with two words: festival atmosphere. This is, however, born of many small things. Paradoxically, one often only understands what these small things are when they are missing from a festival.

I've participated in almost 50 different international film festivals in my life, many of these several times. I've spent some three months of my life at the Annecy animation festival. I've programmed many festivals and even organized a few myself.

Clip from Nourredin ZarrinKelk's film "1, 2, 3, more".

What have I learned from these experiences?

A very important ingredient for the festival atmosphere are the guests. They create the feeling that something is happening. An ambitious festival encourages a healthy, inclusive environment that nurtures social interactions among filmmakers and between filmmakers and the audience.

I was once at an animation festival where, at the beginning of a competition screening, a long list of sponsoring companies was presented, with no mention of the attending filmmakers. In some cases, these directors arrived from other continents just so they could not be introduced with their film. Not good.

Every festival needs some kind of gathering place, usually a cafe where festival visitors can meet each other. Surprisingly, there are festivals that do not tell festival guests which bar or cafe to flock to, a gesture that would not cost them anything. A festival is not only films, it is people. We can watch films at home on the computer, but we cannot meet other people from the world of animation on our living room sofa.

Of course, there should be additional activities alongside the films. Workshops, retrospective screenings, lectures, exhibitions and parties are all regular festival events.

Picnic during the Vranje SAF Workshop 2008.

Ed Hooks presents during
the International Animation
Day Activities 2010.

One shouldn't underestimate the importance of festival parties. One of the legendary festival parties takes place at the Tampere International Short Film Festival in Finland. Guests are invited to a sauna. Those who dare to go are usually very happy they did and, later, spread the word about this most original party.

Even though there are good festivals covering more than one week, I would say that a perfect festival is compact, with a limited length of days. Our physical and mental capacities have natural limits; not many of us have the perseverance to maintain our festival spirit for more than five to six days. In five days, a good programmer can screen a lot of films and even leave festival guests some space for lunch and dinner.

Good festivals take care of the visitors, especially their foreign guests. There should be information available in various languages, someone to answer the questions and enough parties and other gatherings to stimulate socializing.

And yes, one should not forget one thing: a good film program is also essential for a film festival. There are many ways to collect an interesting program—it only needs fresh ideas and some dedicated work.

Heikki Jokinen

Heikki is ASIFA Vice-President and serves as a liaison between ASIFA and festivals.

Taking a break during Zagreb
Animation Festival 1988.

Xiamen Animation
Festival Exhibit
of work by
Bordo Dovnikovic.

Bordo shows off his alcohol filled
bugle bottle during Vranje 2008.

Emanuele Luzzati and Giulio Gianini.

ASIFA Festival Policy

John Halas and Milivoj Pogrmilovic (head of Zagrebfilm) at Mamaia festival 1970.

ASIFA and film festivals have walked hand in hand for a long time. When the Annecy Animation Festival and ASIFA were created, they were essentially two sides of the same coin. ASIFA also has longstanding relationships with other festivals (e.g. Zagreb and Ottawa). In the past ASIFA endorsement was important for an animation festival. An ASIFA supported festival indicated that the event was reliable and respectful to filmmakers.

Things gradually changed after the Cold War ended. ASIFA had played a pivotal role in bringing together East and West animators and their films. With the collapse of the

Iron Curtain and changing screening formats, ASIFA's role with festivals diminished to some degree. Almost anyone could submit their films to festivals. Changing technologies made the process easier and cheaper. Gone were the days of creating and sending expensive 35mm film prints. The creation of VHS, DVDs, and, today, digital formats has made animation festivals more accessible to animators. At the same time, numerous animation festivals emerged. This made it increasingly difficult for ASIFA to evaluate festivals. In time, festivals did not necessarily need the approval of ASIFA.

In 2001, the ASIFA board formulated a new festival policy. We kept the traditional partner festivals (e.g. Annecy, Zagreb, Hiroshima, Ottawa), that have had a long relationship with ASIFA. The status of "partner festival" does not make an exclusive list of the crème de la crème of animation festivals—it simply indicates that the festival and ASIFA have decided to help and promote each other. Of course our "partner festivals" also respect the filmmakers' rights in their regulations and practices. This was and remains a priority for both the festivals and ASIFA.

A major task of ASIFA is to protect the interests of the filmmakers. Helping animators navigate through the sea of animation festivals is an essential part of ASIFA's work. It is absolutely vital for ASIFA that the festivals respect the filmmakers' rights and ensure that rules in competitions and other areas be fair to all competitors.

For this reason the ASIFA board decided to start the festival evaluation system. We drafted a list of criteria including a description of the competitive program, festival promotion and communication, prizes and hospitality for filmmakers in competition.

Our aim was to collect this basic information to the ASIFA web page and, over time, create a database for filmmakers and producers to check how the festival actually is built

JICA 1981, selection committee Clockwise: Henri Gruel (France) - Genevieve Georgescu (Romania) - Joyce Borenstein (Canada) - Paul Demeyer (Belgium).

Fedor Khitruk and Fini Littlejohn (Bill's wife) doing culture at Varna 1979.

Right: ASIFA Board at Budapest 1973 - Gyorgy Matolcsy, Ivan Ivanov-Vano, unidentified, (behind) Miroslav Kijowicz and Max Massimino Garnier.

Bottom: SAF workshop 2005 with Eric Vanz De Godoy (France), Fernado Galrito (Portugal), Frantisek Jurisic (Slovakia) Yuri Krasny (Ukraine), Karine Jeannet (France), James Clay (Austria), Susie Wilson (Scotland).

and organized. Only those festivals that fulfill the basic criteria—like offering any kind of hospitality to filmmakers in competition—were promoted in ASIFA media, our magazine and webpage.

Unfortunately this did not work as well as planned; we are a network of voluntary people. However, on asifa.net we published several festival reports which together form at least one source of information on the festivals. During the recent reshaping of our website, the festival report archive was removed. There are, however, plans to rebuild the festival section.

ASIFA also monitors festival regulations. If we are notified about unfair rules or irregularities, ASIFA will contact the festival to discuss the possible problems and, if necessary, request that they correct their rules.

This is where the ASIFA festival policy stands at the moment. We continue our mutual cooperation with our partner festivals and continue to distribute practical festival information that is relevant to the filmmakers.

Heikki Jokinen

Heikki is ASIFA Vice-President and serves as a liaison between ASIFA and festivals.

ASIFA Board at Xiamen Animation Festival 2009. From left: Hannah, Vesna Dovnikovic, Brett Thompson, Bordo Dovnikovic, Johnchill Lee, Antran Manoogian, Ed Desroches, Nancy Denney- Phelps, Nelson Shin, and Heikki Jokinen.

ACTIVITIES

ASIFA MAGAZINES

2008

2009

2010

Since its foundation in 1961 ASIFA has published a journal which includes, and has included, articles on important ASIFA issues, but also about relevant issues on animation in general. It was published in French, English and Russian as three official ASIFA languages. Today it is printed in English and translated to French and Spanish in digital form.

The journal has moved many times over the years, depending on the editor or publisher of the magazine with any given issue.

First edited in Paris in 1961, this bulletin of modest origins moved to Bucharest, Romania thanks to the financial support given by the Romanian authorities.

Between 1973 and 1977 the journal was published in Budapest, Hungary which was supported by the Hungarian authorities.

The journal has also been published in Poland, Italy, Belgium, Czech Republic and Canada.

Since 1995, CARTOONS and ASIFA Magazine has been published by John Libbey Publishing and edited by Chris Robinson.

Vesna Dovnokovic
ASIFA General Secretary

HISTORY OF ASIFA PERIODICALS

1961 - 1966
Bulletin trimestriel de liaison del'l ASIFA (Fr. Engl. Rus.)
Edited in Paris, France.   Managing Director: Pierre Barbin

1966 - 1972
Bulletin of the International Association of Animated Film ASIFA (Fr. Eng. Rus.)
Edited in Bucharest, Romania.   Editors: Marian Paraianu and Elvira Anitei.

1973 -1977
ANIMAFILM (Fr, Eng. Rus)
Edited in Budapest, Hungary, by Gyorgy Matolcsy

1978 - 1980
ANIMAFILM   (Fr. Engl. Rus.)
Edited in Poland.   Editor: Marcin Gizycki

1981 – 1988
ANIMAFILM, International Quarterly of Animated Film (Fr. Engl. Rus)
Edited in Turin, Italy, by Centro Internazionale per Cinema di Animazione.   Editor: Alfio Bastiancich.

1988 (May) - 1992
ASIFA NEWS   (Fr. Engl. Rus.)
Edited in Bruxelles, Belgium, by Folioscope.   Editors: Doris Cleven, Philippe Moins.

1993 - 2000
ASIFA NEWS (Fr. Eng. Rus).
Edited in Praha, Czech Republic.   Editor: Stanislav Ulver

2001 – 2004
ASIFA MAGAZINE (Fr. Eng. Rus.)
Edited in Ottawa, Canada.   Editor: Chris Robinson

2005 - 2007
CARTOONS (English)
Published by John Libbey Publishing Ltd.   Editor: Chris Robinson

2008 –
ASIFA MAGAZINE, The International Animation Journal (English, online translations to Fr. Sp.)
Published by John Libbey Publishing Ltd.   Editor: Chris Robinson

THE MANY FACES OF

ASIFA PERIODICALS

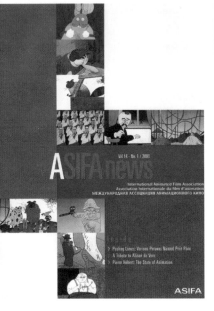

ASIFA WORKSHOPS

ASIFA WORKSHOP GROUP (AWG)

The ASIFA Workshop Group is an international movement represented in 23 countries on 4 continents. Every year an international project is implemented by children.

The history of the children's workshops started in 1971 when it was founded at the Atelier de Cinema d' animation d' Annecy et de Haute Savoie (AAA), by Alexandre Alexeieff and Claire Parker. In 1979, the workshops became officially known as the ASIFA WORKSHOP GROUP (AWG).

Workshop in Thailand.

With all these years of experience, we've discovered that the art of animation is the most common medium for children to express their ideas and overcome language barriers. Through the activities of the AWG, children become a more critical audience and, ideally, staunch supporters of the animation art form.

Children start with simple animation experiments. For example, they might use puppet, clay animation or pixilation to make films of each other. As soon as they see the result of their efforts, they realize that they have been engaged in the art of animation.

They love to tell stories. The artistic mind develops through symbols and metaphors because they include certain images and emotions. We encourage the young animators to tell stories with symbolic meanings to provoke the audience with dramatic techniques.

The art of animation allows children to create unrealistic and physically impossible stories with many adventures. They also have the opportunity to express their ideas on current topics such as the environment, world peace, racism, etc.

The creation of animation movies encourages the children to record their observations and to express their emotions such as friendship, love, satisfaction, loneliness.

Throughout the animation activity, we have noticed that the skills a child animator acquires are:
1. A sensitivity of problems and the ability to distinguish between them.
2. A mental ability to produce ideas derived from various stimulations and to solve problems within a certain timeframe.
3. A mental suppleness that forgoes a routine attitude. The child produces varied solutions. This variety characterizes the flexible mind and presupposes the change.
4. Originality
5. Synthetical skills Their creative minds demand elaborate ideas to be organized in larger schemes with more brevity.
6. Ability to elaborate ideas with the creation of a story.

We are very happy to see in the festivals the animated films made by children and we are very optimistic about the future of animation.

Anastasia Dimitra

Anastasia is from Greece, teaching as well designing animation. She is currently the president of ASIFA Workshops Group and is Treasurer of ASIFA.

Top three pictures from Workshops in Greece.
Bottom picture from workshop in Thailand.

Above: Workshop with
Adrian Petringenaru.
Top: Vranje 2008 Workshop
attendees during picnic.

AWG Creates Something Wonderful in the World

Children are very creative and expressive. They thoroughly enjoy the arts and sciences and to learn and explore. They especially love the process of animation, both the creation and the end result. They love to conjure up stories. They laugh when the images they have created move. And they are completely awed when the entire process is presented back to them on the screen.

With animation, children are able to use their creativity. They are also educated in culture, story writing, critical thinking, math, physics, and so much more during the creation of animation. And the best part is that they love every minute of the process especially when they see their

results spring to life. Nowhere is that process understood more fully than with ASIFA Workshop Groups (AWG). Workshops are a great way to involve children and let their imaginations run wild. Workshops allow the participants to create and critique, opening their minds, while, at the same time, giving them the forum to think critically.

With this in mind, the beginnings of AWG were developed in 1979, backed by then ASIFA president John Halas, the Atelier de Cinéma d'Animation d'Annecy (AAA) and Nicole Solomon. They were inspired by a screening of children's work from AAA based on the theme of childhood. There was a gap to fill for cross-cultural cooperation. Children's animation workshops could fill that gap by providing a link between children from around the world.

A board was then formed for AWG which included Nicole Solomon of AAA, Edo Lukman of Croatia and David Ehrlich of USA. The organization quickly grew from the one studio, AAA, to include many workshops around the globe. What started with a few students now had over 300 students from 16 countries by 1989.

Although animation is typically a fun and fantastic world, the projects that AWG tackles are not always lighthearted. Some of the projects included themes such as pollution, the meaning of love, and children's rights. Projects that tickle their imaginations included those about the moon or a 25th or 50th anniversary. Often, the project requires them to listen to the sound of animation or even traditional children's songs and match the music with the motion. Then there are the Olympics, and twice now the projects have included the Olympics, once for Lillehammer and once for Beijing.

The workshops themselves take on many forms. Some workshops are large studios used only for the children's animation. Others are studios that open their doors to interested children. Still more workshops are based in public

Workshop in Michigan USA
with Deanna Morse.

Workshop in Belgium

and private schools, bringing animation to a more main-stream environment. And yet, there are even the single apprentice-based workshops providing a more intimate process.

Of course, the mediums are just as diverse as the workshops. From cutouts to clay, from sand to stop-motion, drawing, computer 2D and computer 3D, found objects and water color, pixilation and lights, the sky is the limit with techniques used allowing the children to always be excited and curious. Whatever the method, it usually ends up with the same result: fun for the children.

The purpose of the workshops is not to mold children into animators or to make them focus solely on the art. The workshops exist to share the art of animation with the children. They learn quickly that they are dealing with an art that requires both time and skill to produce something special. They learn to be critical of the art and to appreciate the work involved. They learn to work in groups and teams. But mostly they learn that hard work pays off and can be fun and rewarding.

Overall, the process, the techniques, the creativity fold into one thing: the screening. Watching the children as they watch their own magic is its own reward. Dreamy-eyed they sit looking at the screen in a state of awe and often-times smiling or laughing.

AWG Workshop Group.

The workshops have created something wonderful in the world. They bring together children of all races, religions and walks of life. The workshops are building a global community and they are continually growing and making the world a smaller place to share that creativity, imagination and energy.

Ed Desroches

Ed is a Vice President of ASIFA and President of ASIFA-Colorado. Aside from working in animation, digital editing, and web design and development Ed regularly holds children's animation workshops. He is an expert marksman and pacifist along with having a degree in eternal optimism.

from top:
Workshop in Belgium,
Workshop in Austria,
Workshop in China with David Ehrlich,
Workshop in Cakovec with David Ehrlich.

CHRISTEL DEGROS

Interview By Anastasia Dimitra

Christel Degros
onstage during
Hiroshima 2010.

Why are you member of ASIFA?

In 1993, I started working with children in animation workshops.

It was Raoul Servais and Nicole Salomon who introduced us, in Annecy, to Sayoko Kinoshita.

Until that moment I didn't know about the existence of workshops for children in other parts of the world. Soon, we became members of ASIFA and joined AWG.

Although Ghent, Belgium is my home base, I've workshops all over Flanders, together with my colleague, Iza Cracco. We moved around with our equipment (15 years ago it wasn't as compact as now) to schools and events.

I've now been a member for several years, and I have had the pleasure of participating in several AWG projects. The international connection gives me the opportunity to join festivals where one can meet animation friends and encounter new ones. For me, being an ASIFA member means being part of the complete picture.

What connects the members of ASIFA?

ASIFA is the big 'animation family'. It doesn't matter if you're occupied with animation in a professional way or just as a hobby, animation is the common connection.
Animation is fun. Animation can be a serious occupation or avocation. The attraction between the members is the passion for animation. It is the mix of people with different backgrounds, different levels of experience but with the same interests that makes it all worth while.

What do you think about the future of Asifa?

Animation can connect people in different ways, and it does. ASIFA is a great organisation bringing animation people together. It started with a few ambitious and enthusiastic people and it keeps on growing. The spirit of the founders should continue. No political, religious or other backgrounds should keep one from coming together in the world of animation.

Work on The Painted Bird.

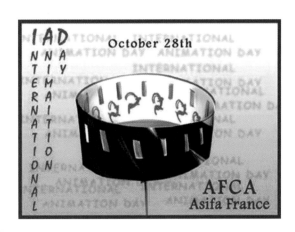

INTERNATIONAL ANIMATION DAY OCTOBER 28TH

"International days", there are already a lot of them and for all kind of things. There is likely not a single day of the year that does not celebrate something. So why not an International animation day as well? What was bugging Abi Feijo, then ASIFA president, when he got such a strange idea?

Maybe this was a good opportunity to pay a tribute to Emile Reynaud, the inventor of animated films? Perhaps animation needed an event to itself, an anchor point beyond the major festivals, something to reach a broader general audience throughout the world? In any case that's how we understood the message here at AFCA: To pay a tribute to Emile Reynaud (with the first show at Musee in Paris where Reynaud used to perform) and to make this event an open public demonstration, in any location, for all kinds of activities for anyone and everyone.

As soon as it started in 2002, the international day quickly received an overwhelming response, moving from three days to five days of festivities in nearly 120 locations all over France. The most prestigious cultural places participated including the French Cinémathèque, George Pompidou center, the Cité des sciences et de l'industrie, Unesco in Paris and even the Senate!… Other countries such as Portugal, Croatia, Romania and India also came on board, creating their own unique celebrations.

In November 2003, a stronger ASIFA renewed its board of directors. To my request, I became in charge of coordinating the event on a global scale. It was a huge challenge, but the French experience provided me with ideal training. Of course, using the different groups from ASIFA across the world was also very helpful. But it became obvious very soon for the interest of the event and the growth of ASIFA that we needed to go beyond a single network. We had to talk to the film festivals, national associations and institutions that may be potentially interested in animation films in order to get what we wanted - a similar process to what we did with the French celebration, but a lot more tedious.

Finding the right interlocutors required a long search, followed by intense discussions to convince them, all those efforts before we saw our first results: 30 countries participating in 2004. Two elements were essential to meet this challenge: First, each organizer had to make the manifestation its own, which included a total freedom of content and shape of the event. ASIFA had to be able support the participants with the strength of its network; if not on a financial level. With that in mind, I offered the idea to publish a program of animated films on DVD to be screened free of rights within the context of the event. I tried to use the Association's network to advertise the event, but, I have to say, that is not ASIFA's greatest strength.

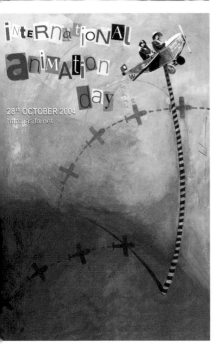

A lot of participants got involved once or twice in a humble way, but other countries turned the celebration into a successful annual event. In France, Portugal and Brazil, International Animation Day has grown into a huge, wide-spread event taking place over several days in many cities. On a smaller scale, happenings such as workshops or screenings in various locations are proof of the success

of the manifestation and give ASIFA its raison d'être. All those actions made it possible to reach new places and a larger public.

Taking a few steps back, I can say that the International Day had many positive effects in general. First, on the ASIFA level, it was the occasion to work with each ASIFA national group, each making their own personal contributions. I have to mention how happy I felt when I saw different groups getting involved in the project, sometimes with a lot of enthusiasm and ground breaking ideas.

This initiative has brought broader attention and recognition to ASIFA in both animation world and more official entities. It also contributed to the birth of several new national ASIFA groups. Finally, it gave a chance for a new audience to discover this unique art form, which, at its core, is what ASIFA is all about.

Today, the International day is alive and doing well, it is

settling down, getting stronger and more structured thanks to the enthusiasm and energy of those who took the torch back.

In fact, Abi, this was not such bad idea, was it?

Olivier Catherin.

Olivier is a member of the board of the French Animated Film Association (AFCA). From 2003 to the beginning of 2008, he was the French representative on the ASIFA board, and was in charge of the coordination of the International Animation Day.

Translated by Laurence Arcadias.

Still from Scurta Istorie by Ion Popescu-Gopo.　　Still from E by Bretislav Pojar.

FILM ARCHIVE

During the Cold War, ASIFA maintained an archive of 16mm and 35mm films in Europe. The materials were made available to educators and others. In the 1980s two or three outstanding 16mm programs from the archive were shown in the U.S. by ASIFA chapters. Today, video copies and DVDs of the works have been included as well.

Tsvika Oren, an animator, animation teacher, festival director, writer and past head of ASIFA Israel, notes that several governments maintained film collections at their embassies: "We often borrowed films from the Czech, German, and other embassies. Canada made available lots of NFB animation. France and UK did too, although there was less emphasis on animation." The United States made films available abroad through the U.S Information Agency.

excerpted from an article by Karl Cohen

Karl is President of ASIFA-San Francisco and an ASIFA Prize winner.

Still from The Exciting Love Story
by Bordo Dovnikovic.

Still from Stowaway by Abi Feijo.

Still from La Belle Fille Et Le Sorcier
by Michel Ocelot.

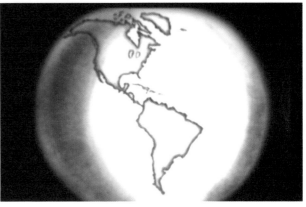

Still from The Mad Mad Mad World
by Noureddin ZarrinKelk.

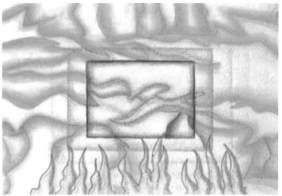

Still from Goldframe by Raoul Servais.   Still from Line Dance by David Ehrlich.

ASIFA PRIZE

Since 1985 ASIFA gives a prize for the outstanding achievements in the art of animation. The ASIFA Prize is awarded
annually to individual(s) or organisation(s) which have
made a significant and innovative contribution towards the
promotion and preservation of the art of animation. This
internationally recognised prize plays an important role in
the animation community.

1985	Kihachiro Kawamoto awarded in Varna
1986	John Halas awarded in Zagreb
1986	Louise Beaudet awarded in Hamilton
1987	Katia (or Katja) Georgi awarded in Annecy
1987	Karel Zeman awarded in Hiroshima
1987	Dusan Vukotic awarded in Varna
1988	Frederic Back awarded in Zagreb

Still from Do It Yourself Cartoon Kit by Bob Godfrey.

Still from Life Without Gabriella Ferri by Priit and Olga Parn.

Still from Bon Voyage Sim by Moustapha Alassane.

1989	Fedor Hitruk awarded in Annecy
1989	Bill Littlejohn awarded in Varna
1990	Daniel Szczechura awarded in Zagreb
1990	Bob Godfrey awarded in Hiroshima
1990	Jan Svankmajer awarded in Ottawa
1991	Paul Grimault awarded in Annecy
1992	Nicole Salomon awarded in Hiroshima
1993	Yoji Kuri awarded in Annecy
1994	Paul Driessen awarded in Ottawa
1995	Te Wei awarded in Annecy
1996	Bretislav Pojar awarded in Zagreb
1998	The Quay Brothers awarded in Zagreb
1999	Clare Kitson awarded in Espinho
2000	Jules Engel, Rene Jodoin awarded in Ottawa
2001	Priit Parn awarded in Ottawa
2002	David Ehrlich awarded in Zagreb
2004	Bruno Edera, Raoul Servais, June Foray awarded in Annecy, Zagreb, Hiroshima
2006	Normand Roger awarded in Hiroshima
2007	Margit Antauer awarded in Annecy
2008	Karl Cohen awarded in Ottawa
2009	Moustapha Allasane awarded in Accra

OUR
CHAPTERS

ASIFA ARGENTINA

Quirino Cristiani.

November 9, 1917, twenty years before the production of Snow White by Walt Disney, marked the debut of Argentine animation with the screening of the feature animated film The Apostle, a satire on the government's first Argentine president elected by popular vote: Don Hipólito Irigoyen.

The author of the film was Quirino Cristiani. Emigrating with his family from Italy at the age of four, Cristiani devoted himself to drawing and, at the age of 18, he was already a recognized cartoonist and political humorist. His drawings appeared in the Argentine Events Weekly Newsreel, until he turned to animation and made The Apostle.

Drawing of The Apostle.

Cristiani's work influenced many young artists to embrace animation. In a market that was beginning to be dominated by Hollywood films, a new crop of animators made many short and feature length animations for Argentine theatres.

During the '40s and '50s, the presence of national characters in cinemas in the country was possible thanks to the advertising films with animated drawings. They also occupied the screen in B / N of the first state TV channel, opened in 1952.

Top: Young Q Cristiani in his Animation Stand surrounded by cuttings.
Middle: RAID still Desplats studio.
Bottom: Mafalda still Desplats studio.

In the '60s, the opening of three private air channels exponentially increased the advertising market, with a demand that enabled a new generation of illustrators and animators. This new generation transformed into entrepreneurs, founding the first permanent animation studios in Buenos Aires, and among them was my own studio: Story Productions. We replaced our own productions with cartoons imported from U.S.A. by advertising agencies. Later our advertising animation also supplied a huge number of local customers.

At the same time, the colour versions of these commercials monopolized the Theatres' screens of our country and its neighbours. At the end of the '60s, the advertising animation stopped being a testing ground and became a professional discipline that started the production of indigenous TV series with Argentine characters.

Already in the '70s, these studios, with teams of Argentine animators transformed into professionals by simple transmission of knowledge through their pioneer teachers, resumed the production of animated entertainment. In 1972, 45 years after the invention of Q. Cristiani, Argentina's first colour animated feature film, One Thousand Attempts and One Invention by the producer Garcia Ferre.

In 1978, the Animation Filmmakers Argentine Association (AARCA) was founded. Its goals were inspired by ASIFA, but in this first entity AARCA only admitted cartoon artists and animation professionals. The Association adopted as logo, "Isotype", the main character from The Apostle, "as a tribute to the pioneer Cristiani". Lectures, free and public screenings of films made by international animators were screened courtesy of various embassies. There were also tributes to pioneers like Dante Quinterno, Manuel García Ferre and Victor Iturralde Rúa.

In 2003, ASIFA-International began the International Animation Day on October 28 of each year. Argentine animation celebrated International Animation Day with the

"New Approach Association, for Children and Youth". In 2005, the event was included in the "4th International Film Festival for Children and Youth", where I was curator of the Animation Exhibition.

This included projections and various acts, and the colloquium "Meeting between Animators", that brought together artists and technicians, independent and industry animators. During this event, we discussed the idea of reshaping the Animation Film Association. Olivier Catherin, president of ASIFA France, suggested the possibility of creating ASIFA-Argentina.

In 2006, twenty animation artists and technicians formed an organizing committee with two objectives: first, to raise the funds necessary to carry out the acts of the International Animation Day; second, to found A.A.C.A. the Argentine Film Animation Association. On 28 October, at the Center of Exhibitions El Dorrego, assigned by the government of the City of Buenos Aires, both objectives were met.

We performed our 1st Animation Exhibition of independent shorts, films and national TV Series in the process of production, student films and other events. During the main symposium, "Animators Meeting", the new association A.A.C.A. was officially launched.

Above: One thousand attempts and one invention still Garcia Ferre studio.

A.A.R.C.A. Directive Committee Photography 1978. From left to right: U. Galuppo, M.Nanni, C.Berrino, J.Martin, A. del Castillo, R.Lamponi, O.M. Desplats, N.Gaite y L.Cedr in 1978.

A.A.C.A. immediately began seeking the recognition of ASIFA-International with the invaluable help of its General Secretary, Vesna Dovnikovic. A.A.C.A. adopted the same objectives and adapted the statute of ASIFA-International. Once the negotiation was done, with the recommendation of Jordi Artigas, from ASIFA Barcelona, Olivier Catherin of ASIFA-France, and Oscar Grillo, a famous Argentine animator and a personal friend, A.A.C.A. was designated ASIFA-Argentina on February 14, 2007.

On April 23, 2007, the twenty founding members signed the Constitutive Act of A.A.C.A. The draft of the statutes was read and approved and the first directive committee elected was for three years. ASIFA-Argentina was officially born.

Inspired by the same objectives of ASIFA, we are trying to encourage young people to engage and embrace animation, fulfilling the mandate left to us, more than 90 years ago, by the pioneering animators in Argentina.

Oscar M. Desplats

Oscar is animation producer, director and profesor, founder and President of AACA- ASIFA Argentina.

From left to right: R. Pastor, S.Nanni, O.M.Desplats, R.Manfredi y M.Nanni.

A.S.I.F.A. ARGENTINA: CUMPLIENDO EL MANDATO DE LOS PIONEROS

Por Oscar M. Desplats – Presidente A.A.C.A.- A.S.I.F.A. Argentina

Sabe Ud. que el primer Largometraje animado del mundo se realizo y estreno en Buenos Aires, capital de la República Argentina, ubicada en el extremo Sur del continente americano?

El 9 de Noviembre de 1917, veinte años antes de la producción de Blanca Nieves por Walt Disney, se estreno el filme animado "El apóstol", de una hora de duración, cuyo argumento era una sátira sobre el gobierno del primer presidente argentino elegido por voto popular: Don Hipólito Irigoyen.

El autor del filme se llamaba Quirino Cristiani. Emigrado con su familia desde Italia a la edad de 4 años, se dedico al dibujo y a la temprana edad de 18 años ya era dibujante y humorista político reconocido. Sus caricaturas fijas aparecían en el Noticiero semanal Sucesos Argentinos, hasta que encontró la manera de darles movimiento. Dibujó y articuló las siluetas de sus personajes y luego las filmo, cuadro por cuadro, mediante su sistema patentado, dando nacimiento al largometraje "El Apostol", que tuvo mucho éxito y se exhibió durante más de un año. Quirino Cristiani ocupa un lugar destacado en la galería de los pioneros del mundo de la animación.

La animación argentina siguió desarrollándose con el trabajo de los colaboradores de Cristiani y de los dibujantes que aprendieron a animar con ellos, logrando mantener en los cines la exhibición de dibujos animados de corto y largometraje, en un mercado que empezaba a ser dominado por la producción de Hollywood.

Durante la década del 40 y 50, la presencia de personajes nacionales en los cines del país fue posible gracias a los dibujos animados publicitarios. Estos ocuparon también la pantalla en B/N del primer canal de TV, estatal, inaugurado a fines de 1951.

Ya en la década del '60, la apertura de tres canales de aire privados aumento exponencialmente el mercado publicitario, con una demanda que permitio que apareciera una nueva generación de Dibujantes-Animadores. Ellos mismos, transformados en empresarios, fundaron los primeros estudios permanentes de animación en Bs Aires, y entre ellos estaba mi propio estudio: Producciones Story. Los filmes provenientes de U.S.A. para publicitar a los clientes internacionales de las agencias de publicidad argentinas, fueron reemplazados por nuestra propia producción. La animación publicitaria abastecio también a una enorme cantidad de clientes locales.

A su vez, las versiones en color de estos comerciales, monopolizaron las pantallas cinematográficas de nuestro país y de sus vecinos, en forma de multitud de copias 35 mm color, cuya exhibición reinstauro el circuito perdido por la animación desde mediados de los años '50.-. A fines de los años 60, la animación publicitaria dejo de ser un campo de experimentación para transformarse en una disciplina profesional que inicio la producción de Series unitarias de TV de un minuto diario, con personajes argentinos cuyo éxito perdura hoy dia.

Ya en la década del 70, estos estudios, con planteles de animadores argentinos transformados en profe sionales mediante la simple transmisión del conocimiento de sus maestros pioneros, reiniciaron la producción de animación de entretenimiento, y en 1972, 45 años después del invento de Q.Cristiani, se estreno por fin el primer largometraje animado en color de producción nacional, el dibujo animado" Mil intentos y un invento", de la Productora Garcia Ferre.

LOS ANIMADORES PIONEROS FUNDAN LA PRIMERA ASOCIACION: A.A.R.C.A.
Esta relevancia de la animación hizo posible el nacimiento, en 1978, de la primera Asociación, A.A.R.C.A.: sigla que significaba Asociación Argentina de Realizadores de Cine de Animación. Sus objetivos se inspiraron en los de A.S.I.F.A., la Asociación Internacional del Cine de Animación, pero en esta primera entidad solamente se admitía como socios a

Poster of The Apostle.
From left to right R.W.Desplats, S.Nanni and O.M.Desplats.

artistas del dibujo animado y técnicos de cámara y edición que trabajaban profesional mente en la anima¬ción de la época: el dibujo en lápiz y el calco en acetato, ambos a mano, con el estilo de Disney como paradigma.

La Asociación adopto como Logo-Isotipo el personaje del film "El Apostol", como homenaje al pionero Q. Cristiani. Sin embargo, debido a la declinación del mercado de animación publicitaria, esta Asociación tuvo una vida corta aunque útil al fin. Se realizaron conferencias, proyecciones gra¬tuitas y de difusión general, en la época en que los filmes de animadores internacionales se conseguían por gentileza de las embajadas. También se realizaron actos de reconocimiento a pioneros como Dante Quinterno, Manuel García Ferre y Víctor Iturralde Rúa, por sus ejemplares trayectorias.

1ra CELEBRACION DEL DIA INTERNACIONAL DE LA ANIMACION EN Bs Aires.
A.S.I.F.A. Internacional inicio en el 2003 la celebración del DIA INTERNACIONAL de la ANIMACION el 28 de Octubre de cada año. En el año 2005, la Asociación "Nueva Mirada" de nuestro país tomó a su cargo la realización de la celebración por primera vez, incluyéndolo en el "4to Festival de Cine para la Infancia y la Juventud" donde fui curador de la Muestra de Animación. Esta incluyo proyecciones y actos varios, y el coloquio "Encuentro entre animadores", que reunió a los artistas y técnicos independientes y de la industria.

Durante este acto instalamos la idea de refundar la Asociación de Cine de Animación y Olivier Catherine, presidente de A.S.I.F.A. Francia, enterado del éxito obtenido, sugirió la posibilidad de crear A.S.I.F.A. Argentina.

LOS ANIMADORES SE HACEN CARGO
En el año 2006, veinte artistas y técnicos de la animación, formaron una Comisión Organizadora con dos objetivos, primero: reunir los fondos necesarios para llevar a cabo los actos del Día Internacional de la Animación y segundo: fundar A.A.C.A. la Asociación Argentina de Cine de Animación.

El 28 de Octubre, en el Centro de Exposiciones El Dorrego,

Anteojito still Garcia Ferre studio.

cedido por el gobierno de la Ciudad de Bs Aires se cumplieron ambos objetivos. Se realizo nuestra 1ra Muestra de Animación, de cortos independientes, de Filmes y Series TV nacionales en proceso de producción, de filmes de estudiantes y del programa ¨Caloi en su tinta¨, Incluimos Animadores trabajando en vivo y Debates, actos que contaron con gran concurrencia de profesionales y estu¬diantes del medio y de público aficionado. Durante el coloquio principal, el ¨Encuentro de animadores¨, y ante una audiencia que aplaudió la iniciativa, se produjo el lanzamiento de la nueva asociación A.A.C.A.

A.A.C.A. - A.S.I.F.A. ARGENTINA SEÑALA EL CAMINO

Autorizada por la Inspección General de Justicia del estado nacional, A.A.C.A. inició la tramitación del reconocimiento como Grupo ante A.S.I.F.A. Internacional con la ayuda invalorable de su Secretaria general, Vesna Dovnikovic. Adopto los mismos objetivos y adecuo su Estatuto al de A.S.I.F.A. internacional.

Concluida la gestión con la recomendación de Jordi Artigas, de ASIFA Barcelona, del propio Olivier Catherin, de ASIFA Francia y de Oscar Grillo, famoso animador argentino y amigo personal, A.A.C.A. fue designada A.S.I.F.A. Argentina el 14 de Febrero de 2007.

El 23 de Abril de 2007, en un acto-asamblea público los Veinte miembros fundadores firmaron el Acta constitutiva de A.A.C.A., se leyó y aprobó el proyecto de Estatuto y la primera Comisión Direc¬tiva electa por tres años, anunció el comienzo de las actividades de la asociación. Entre ellas la celebración anual del Día Internacional de la Animación el 28 de Octubre, que venimos haciendo en forma ininterrumpida desde hace ya cinco años. Son pocos, comparados con el cincuentenario de la fundación de A.S.I.F.A. o con los cumplidos por muchos otros Grupos nacionales que nos ayudan con su experiencia. Pero inspirados en los mismos objetivos, estamos tratando de señalar el camino a seguir a una gran cantidad de jóvenes que sueñan con y gracias a la animación, cumpliendo el mandato que nos dejaron, hace mas de 90 años, los animadores pioneros de la Argentina.

ASIFA AUSTRIA

ASIFA-Austria was founded in 1985 by students of the "Studio for Experimental Animation" at the University of Fine Arts in Vienna. The Masterclass for Painting, under the leadership of Maria Lassnig, had opened this unique studio for animation just two years earlier. Hubert Sielecki, leader of that studio since its foundation, played an important role in the foundation of ASIFA-Austria. He also served as the first ASIFA-Austria President from 1985 – 1992. In the first years, the ASIFA-Austria studio was used exclusively by the Academy Students as a meeting place and production centre for animated films. One of the central activities of the first years was the animation school workshops.

In 1992, Thomas Renoldner followed Hubert Sielecki as president of ASIFA-Austria and served in this capacity until 2003. During this period many important initiatives were realized: the technical expansion of the animation studio; the expansion of animation workshops; research and publication projects about the history of animation in Austria; the foundation of an archive for Austrian and international animation (films, video-tapes, books, catalogues,…).

Besides all these activities, the ASIFA Studio, with its 35mm animation stand, was used to produce numerous animated films of ASIFA Austria members.

Since 2003 Stefan Stratil has been the President of ASIFA-Austria. Since that time the activities of ASIFA in the field of presentation and promotion have expanded, while the number of animation workshops have decreased.

Today's main activities of ASIFA-Austria are:
-"ASIFA-Keil": art exhibition at the famous "Museumsquartier", focusing on the dialogue between Fine Arts and animation. (monthly).
-"One Day Animation Festival": ASIFA-Austria's annual animation event on occasion of the International Animation Day at the cinema 'Filmcasino'. (beginning of November).
-"Animation Avantgarde": International Competition and special programmes for the Vienna Independent Short Filmfestival (end of May).
-"Trickplattform": Regular film screening in ASIFA-Austria Studio.

In 2010, a book about animation in Austria was published in collaboration with the Austrian Film Archive.

Future projects include:
- DVD collection about the History of animation in Austria (in collaboration with the Film Archive).
- Expansion of the Animation Archive.
- Technical modernization of the animation production studio.

Opposite and Below: Photos of the ASIFA-Austria studio and members.

Text by ASIFA-Austria

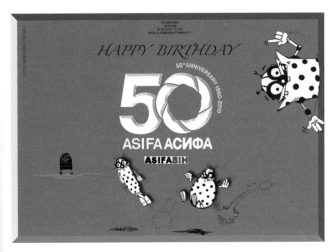

ASIFA BOSNIA AND HERZEGOVINA

ASIFA Bosnia and Herzegovina has existed for six years as a member of ASIFA International. We are very proud to announce that there are two festivals of animated films each year in Bosnia and Herzegovina – in Banja Luka and Neum.

ASIFA-Bosnia and Herzegovina organize International Animation Day in 13 cities all over Bosnia and Herzegovina, with one simple mission - to bring the joy of animated films to all fans and film lovers.

All pictures of ASIFA-Bosnia and Herzegovina IAD celebration in 2008.

Thanks to our friends, and other members of ASIFA, we manage to prepare a selection of best world animated films – due to an exchange we organized during the year.

Every year we celebrate our birthday – the 6th of June – with special screenings and concerts. Each of these celebration parties is followed by workshops for young animators. So far, we have managed to produce some projects that were born during these workshops.

Berin Tuzlic

Berin is President of ASIFA-BiH.

ASIFABIH

Todor Dinov and Feodor Khitruk.

ASIFA BULGARIA

Mr Todor Dinov, a renowned Bulgarian artist and cartoonist and creator of Contemporary Bulgarian professional animation, was one of the founders of ASIFA International. Since then he was the Bulgarian representative in the Board of ASIFA. Later Stoyan Dukov, another famous animated film director was appointed on this position.

Thanks to Mr.Dinov, during the International Animated Film Festival in Mamaia, Romania, in 1970, where a big collection of Bulgarian animated films received the FIPRESSI Award, there was taken the decision to found an ASIFA Bulgaria Chapter, officially established the following year. Pencho Bogdanov, the author of the fabulous "Jolly Fellows", was elected as President of ASIFA Bulgaria.

During the years this new organisation helped to attract many talented writers, poets, artists and composers into the Animated Film Studio "Sofia". There were productions of a great number of significant works, which, thanks to ASIFA-Bulgaria, were presented abroad and had critics speaking about Bulgarian School of Animated Film.

ASIFA-Bulgaria played a very active role on an international scale too. Some of the ASIFA General Assemblies took place in Bulgaria. ASIFA Bulgaria was also one of the organizers of the World Animated Film Festival in Varna in 1979. During an ASIFA meeting there, Bulgaria proposed for the first time the idea for ASIFA Membership Cards.

Nowadays, ASIFA-Bulgaria continues to be an active ASIFA group regularly participating in IAD and the DVD Exchange Programme, making a great number of constructive proposals towards a better future of the association, writing reports and articles for ASIFA Magazine, taking part in the juries of many festivals in the world, organizing animation projections in collaboration with Bulgarian Film Archives and other Cultural Institutions, as well as playing an important role to solve different problems of Bulgarian Animation. Pencho Kunchev was the only Bulgarian representative in ASIFA elected as its Vice President from 2006-2009.

Pencho Kunchev

Pencho is President of ASIFA Bulgaria and previous ASIFA Vice President.

ASIFA CANADA

In 1960, a group of animators felt the need to dedicate their energies to protecting, preserving, and encouraging the art of animated film. It was thus that the Association Internationale du Film d'Animation was formed in France under the presidency of Norman McLaren.

Canada became involved in 1968 through the support of the Cinémathèque Québécoise (known then as the Cinémathèque Canadienne), which proposed to become the North American representative of ASIFA and offered its offices as headquarters.

Neighbours by Norman McLaren.

Canada was also one of the first countries to form its own national chapter, ASIFA-Canada. The first general meeting took place on May 14, 1970. Thirty-eight members elected a Board of Directors consisting of Françoise Jaubert (President), Gerald Potterton (Vice-President), Louise Beaudet (Treasurer), Robert Verrall, Al Sens, Pierre Moretti, Hubert Tison, Michael Mills, Henry Orenstein and Mino Bonan, Board members. Because of the limited number of members, and initially, precarious finances; the Board had to find a way of developing the Association. The Canada Council came to the rescue with a seed grant of $3,000 in 1973. With this support, ASIFA-Canada could not merely operate but flourish. The first newsletter was published on April 24, 1974 and on December 1 of the same year; a small festival was organized with George Dunning and Evelyn Lambart as special guests.

The administrative structure, which had been fairly haphazard until then, was adjusted and formalized through the legal incorporation of the Association on September 30, 1981.

The first major event organized by ASIFA-Canada was a workshop on the occasion on the brand new Ottawa

Festival 76. Co Hoedeman, Huguette Baril, John Gaug, Joyce Borenstein and Inni Karine Melbye were at the heart of the project. The workshop was tremendously successful and outstanding for the calibre of the participants, among them Alexeieff, Lotte Reiniger, Claire Parker, Jules Engel, Norman McLaren, Jacques Drouin, Caroline Leaf, Lynn Smith, Pierre Hébert, Grant Munro and many others.

Our participation in this festival has been constant, despite its relocation to Toronto and Hamilton, and has grown with the years. Under the direction of the President Co Hoedeman, a new activity was devised for Ottawa 78. It was a special rendezvous called CHEZ ANI, where all filmmakers and festival goers could meet, screen films and enjoy themselves in a relaxed atmosphere between official screenings. Once again this event was so popular that it became a tradition. That first year, the organizers of CHEZ ANI started a vote for the public's favourite film. A second ballot was required to choose THE best film of the festival. Ishu Patel's Afterlife won the Chez Ani Grand Prize, followed by SATIMANIA (Z. Gasparovic), Rip Van Winkle (W. Vinton), The Sand Castle (C. Hoedeman) and Pencil Booklings (K. Rose). Each winner received an award in the form of a sculpted snail resembling an animator holding a pencil and carrying his own house, symbolizing the laborious work of animation. This tradition continued from festival to festival, except that only one prize is now awarded. The snails have been replaced by a thaumatrope in a little box.

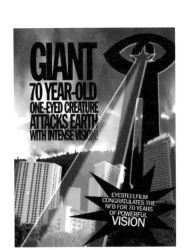

On the occasion of its tenth anniversary, ASIFA-Canada took over the planning of an exceptional picnic. In 1982, the additional responsibility of designing the trophies was bestowed on us. Evelyn Lambart created magnificent banners for the occasion, inspired by the imagery in both her own films and those of Norman MCLaren.

1979 was another memorable year. In cooperation with the Cinémathèque Québécoise and the NFB Festivals Office, ASIFA presented three days of international films entitled Ladies and Gentlemen… Animation at the Outremont

Theatre in Montreal and the Cartier Cinema in Quebec city. An impressive selection of some 160 films divided into twelve programmes was presented to the public and 4,269 people attended. The time-consuming preparations involved the efforts of an organizing committee made up of Jacques Drouin, Hélène Tanguay, Robert Bélisle, Gaston Sarault and Louise Beaudet.

Of the various presentations of all kinds made to the members and the public alike, three exhibitions were truly outstanding: one on animation in the Netherlands (1985), the homage to Norman McLaren following his death in 1987 and the exhibit of drawings from films by Nicole Van Goethem, who personally opened the event (1988). Film screenings accompanied these three exhibitions.

We have almost lost track of the many special screenings organized mainly with the Cinémathèque québécoise; however we recall over forty artists who have honoured us with their presence during these events. Among these were Yuri Norstein, Fiodor Khitruk, Zlatko Grgic, Lou Bunin, Bob Clampett, Jules Engel, Jerzy Kucia and Piotr Dumala. Our own filmmakers, Pierre Hébert, Joyce Borenstein, Normand Roger, Pierre Veilleux, Jean-Thomas Bédard, Donald McWilliams and Norman McLaren, were also honoured.

On two occasions, the Montreal Festival of New Cinema has asked for our assistance. In 1982 when the Festival invited Mary Ellen Bute, a pioneer of abstract animation into the United States, we were given the pleasant duty of receiving her and arranging her Montreal itinerary which she was visiting for the first time at the age of 78. The following year, we organized and programmed the Len Lye retrospective as part of the same festival.

The newsletter, which began as only a few pages, doubled, then tripled its size over the years and became a real magazine. While we applaud this transformation, we must not lose sight of the ongoing work involved in its publication.

Hélène Tanguay and the contributors can testify to this. However the reward comes in the widespread recognition the magazine has received.

Twenty years of continued effort have helped our association flourish, through there has been a cost attached to all of this. The Canada Council has supported us faithfully and has never disappointed us throughout the last seventeen years. Apart from this annual grant, we have received periodic support, either in the form of grants for special projects or as direct financial aid in certain instances, from the Department of External Affairs, Telefilm Canada, the ministère des affaires culturelles (Quebec), and the NFB Communications division through the director of the time, Roland Ladouceur. The French Animation Studio at the NFB has provided us with internal services for several years and maintains a budget for this purpose. The Cinémathèque québécoise graciously allows us to use its screening room and its lobby for our exhibitions. ASIFA-Canada is indeed fortunate.

We can never adequately thank those agencies without whose support our Canadian chapter could barely have survived.

Lastly, I would like to evoke the memory of our honorary president, Norman Mclaren who passed away on the same day as our general meeting in 1987, and to salute René Jodoin, who has assumed that role. ASIFA-Canada can proudly count these two among its own.

Louise Beaudet (courtesy of Helene Tanguay)
October 1990

Postscript:
ASIFA-Canada's decline was relatively quick and painful. With the collapse of support from various institutions, loss of membership and an increasing feeling that ASIFA-Canada was serving on Montreal animators, the organization followed the tumbleweeds.
Chris Robinson

ASIFA CHINA

ASIFA-China was founded on August 29th, 2007. Mr. Chang Guangxi, arrangement principal of ASIFA-China and a well-known animation artist of China, with Mr. Lee Johnchill, senior animator, were delegated to undertake the work of promotion and development of ASIFA in China.

China has a long history with ASIFA. In the 1980s, there were more than 10 Chinese members of ASIFA, including famous animation artists such as Te Wei, Zhang Songlin, A Da, Yan Dingxian, Qian Yunda, Lin Wenxiao, Hu Jinqin, Dai Tielang, Chang Guangxi, Zhou Keqin, Ma Kexuan, Qu Jianfang, Wang Borong, etc. These people assisted in the creation of the international animation film of Shanghai in 1988 and 1992, the first and second international art education forum, and so on. The famous Shanghai Animation Film Studio - which laid the foundation for Chinese animation arts - also participated in many activities held by ASIFA. Legendary animator, Mr. Te Wei, has also won the Lifetime Achievement Award of ASIFA.

ASIFA members in Jilin Institution.

On Oct. 28th, 2010, in order to celebrate the birth of the International Animation Day, ASIFA-CHINA, in

collaboration with the Beijing Film Academy and Shanghai Animation Film Studio, initiated a massive celebration of the state animation industry. This is a response to the first public performance at Theatre Optique. This was held by ASIFA to commemorate the father of the world animation, Emile Reynaud. After that, Oct. 28th has been deemed as the International Animation Day each year ever since. During each International Animation Day, ASIFA-CHINA will go on celebrating it by uniting various people in the animation industry and initiating activities with different subjects like Animation 24 Hours, Special Animation Display, Animation Salon, Animation Dream, etc.

ASIFA-China seeks to, under the righteous guidance of ASIFA, initiate activities like domestic and foreign service coordination, international communication, academic research, information propagation and inquiry service with international animation institutions and animation workers; provide opportunities for domestic animation industries to enter international markets and participate in international competitions, with the ultimate aim of promoting the development of the animation industry in China and throughout the world.

Johnchill Lee

Johnchill is President of ASIFA-China.

IAD screening.

Johnchill Lee signing his name.

ASIFA CROATIA

ASIFA-Croatia is one of the oldest national chapters of ASIFA. Before Croatia became an independent state, this chapter was active as a part of ASIFA-Yugoslavia.

When it was first formed, ASIFA-Croatia consisted entirely of the artists and employees of Zagreb Film, then the biggest animation studio in Croatia. Zagreb Film also took part in the foundation of the World Festival of Animated Film in Zagreb. The manager of Zagreb Film Mr. Jurica Peruzović was also Vice President of the first ASIFA Board of Directors in 1961 (with Norman McLaren as President).

In 2003, the members decided to found an independent association based on the new ASIFA Statutes, so it's been

Top: Bordo Dovnikovic cartoon.
Bottom: Members of ASIFA-Croatia: sitting from left - Margit Buba Antauer, Vesna Dovnikovic, Jasmina Gudic, Ana Marija Vidakovic, standing from left - Ivan Cacic, Stiv Šinik, Željko Kolaric, Bordo Dovnikovic, Ibrahim Bajko Hromalic, Davor Medjurecan, Saša Zec, Marko Meštrovic.

EXCITING LOVE STORY by Bordo Dovnikovic, Special Jury Prize Annecy 1989.

exactly seven years since ASIFA-Croatia has been officially registered as an independent non-profit organization in Croatia.

Some renowned young filmmakers have joined the Group, so ASIFA-Croatia is now a chapter which gathers the most respectable authors of all generations – from famous masters of the golden age of Zagreb animation such as Bordo Dovniković and Pavao Štalter, to younger award-winning filmmakers such as Simon B. Narath, Milan Trenc, Darko Bakliza and others.

At the ASIFA-Croatia party during Annecy Animation Festival 2010, Vesna Dovnikovic and Nelson Shin.

ASIFA-Croatia organizes regular monthly screenings of animated films at the Film Club in Zagreb. Four members of ASIFA-Croatia are members of the Council of World Festival of Animated Film in Zagreb and are involved in organizing this long-standing, world renowned event. ASIFA Croatia has organized the celebrations of the International Animation Day since 2003. In 2010, ASIFA Croatia launched the first national animated film festival in Zagreb and VAFI, international festival of films made by children in Varaždin.

Vesna Dovniković

Vesna is ASIFA Secretary General and President of ASIFA Croatia, she is also a festival organiser and a member of the Board of World Festival of Animated Films in Zagreb.

ALBUM by Kresinir Zimonic, First Prize for Debut, Annecy 1983.

LEVIATHAN, by Simon B. Narath, laureat of the Prize GRAND OFF for the best animation in one European independent film (Warsaw 2007).

ASIFA HRVATSKE

ASIFA Hrvatske jedna je od najstarijih nacionalnih grupa ASIFA-e. Autori i menadžeri Zagreb-filma sudjelovali su u njenom osnivanju i obavljali rukovodeće funkcije u Upravnim odborima ASIFA-e već od samog početka 1961.

Danas ASIFA Hrvatske djeluje kao neprofitna udruga i okuplja značajna imena hrvatskog animiranog filma svih generacija.

Njeni članovi sudjeluju u organizaciji i upravljanju Svjetskim festivalom animiranih filmova u Zagrebu, a 2010. pokrenuli su prvi nacionalni festival animiranog filma u Zagrebu i VAFI, festival dječjeg stvaralaštva u Varaždinu.

Renowned directors of Zagreb School of Animation in 1979.
Standing from left: Zlatko Bourek, Dušan Vukotic, Fadil Hadžic, Aleksandar Marks, Boris Kolar.
Sitting from left: Nedeljko Dragic, Bordo Dovnikovic, Pavao Štalter.

ASIFA EGYPT

On the 4th of March, the Board of ASIFA elected an Egyptian animator to create the poster for the 10th International Animation Day 2011—their first time choosing an artist from Africa to achieve that honour.

This election has symbolic meaning, and not only because of the fact that Ihab Shaker (b. Cairo, 1933) —the chosen artist—is really a great artist, or just in solidarity with the peaceful victory of the Egyptian revolution of January 25, against the dictatorship, which was described by President Obama as "inspiring". On top of all this, an Egyptian was elected to design the annual poster of the international day of the animated art to commemorate the 75th anniversary of Egyptian animation, celebrating the first public showing of locally-made animation in the whole of Africa.

Egypt is the undisputed pioneer in animated films in African countries, as it is in other artistic disciplines related to the audiovisual sector, notably cinema, where we see the important legacy that was left to us more than 100 years ago. Likewise, Egypt is the leader in production, and its audiovisual landscape is more developed than the other countries in its geographical and cultural extent.
Nevertheless, its animation did not succeed in gaining as much notoriety as the Egyptian television series and live-action movies did, for instance, which are enjoyed by millions of households in Arabic countries.

But the story takes place far away from now, that after less than nine years after the creation of the iconic Mickey

IAD in Alexandria

Workshop in Ghana.

IAD in Tunisia.

Mouse, there was a family of craftsmen in the opposite part of the world, in Cairo, who succeeded to show their first animated film to the public in 1936. Back to the roots, in the late 1914, the Byelorussian Frenkel family immigrated to Alexandria, Egypt, to get work, safety, and before all, the freedom from the intolerant Anti-Semitic atmosphere that occurred in the early 20th century in Europe. The family saw Walt Disney animation for the first time in 1930 in Egypt and, at once, they decided to create the Egyptian version of Mickey Mouse even while no one in the family knew anything about making films!

The Frenkel brothers worked hard until they agreed on the character they created - the result was "Marco Monkey", which was criticized by their neighbours because of an evident similarity of the sketches of Walt Disney's hero. The family was advised by one of their friends to find inspiration in the Egyptian culture, native customs and finally created a traditional character, an Egyptian Betty Boop! Still, the Frenkels faced reluctance from prospective clients to place trust in such novices, compared to the talented and prosperous American productions distributed in Egypt. One day back from a meeting, with one of potential producers, quite disappointed, one son of Frenkels' tells, "After Mr. B. listened to me, he said, 'Mafish fayda!' (No way out, dead end). As I tried to insist, he added, 'Bokra fel mish-mish' ("when pigs fly")".

Rather than destroy their determination, this worked as an incentive for the Frenkel brothers to create a new character soon. The name of "Mish-Mish Effendi" came quite naturally to their mind. Then it occurred obvious to title the next film "Mafish fayda". The film was screened in Cairo on February, 8 1936, at the Cosmograph cinema.

Giannalberto Bendazzi, the animation historian described it in his book (Cartoons), "Although the film was not very well drawn, was very badly animated and with an even worse script, the public's enthusiasm through laughs and applause was heard from the outside."

Mish-Mish and the Frenkels became so popular that they were able to start a successful advertising agency. They managed to succeed in mixing Mish-Mish Effendi in the same film with real actors, realizing some short sequences in which Mish-Mish Effendi is dancing in front of a singer and belly dancer.

Almost at the same time, Antoine Selim Ibrahim (1911-1989) made his first film Aziza and Youness in 1938, which is considered to be the first animated film done by an Arabian. That film was followed by Dokdok (1940) and more commercials and titles for live-action movies. Selim emigrated to the USA in 1972 to work at Hanna and Barbara's studio. Bendazzi described in his paper on "African Cinema Animation" the case of animation in Egypt after the immigration of the Frenkel family to France, in the early 1950s, due to the unrest in the Middle East: "Film animation in Egypt saw a renaissance thanks to Ali Moheeb and his brother Husam, who gave birth to the Animation Department within the national television channel which was inaugurated in 1960. In 1962 Ali Moheeb directed The White Line, a film animation plus twenty-five-minute live action, which was a cross between a short musical and a documentary film. It was a lively and excellent film, which made fine use of the split-screen technique (unusual at that time). After eight years of work at the Department, during which he trained many young colleagues, Ali Moheeb successfully switched to advertising. In 1979

Shaker with his wife in his studio with
ASIFA members from Egypt, Sudan,
Tunisia, Lebanon.

Maya Yonesho workshop with ASIFA
Egypt members- Morocco 2011

IAD in South Africa.

ASIFA Prize 2009 of Moustapha Alassane, presented by Mohamed Ghazala in ANIMAFRIK –Ghana.

he directed the first Arab animation film series, 'Mishgias Sawah', composed of thirty episodes for Saudi TV". When Egyptian TV appeared in the 1960s there was an animation department for producing film titles and ads. Some of the great artists worked in this department, contributing to the revolution of animation in Egypt with short films, such as Mohammed Hassib (1937-2001), Noshi Iskandar (Cairo, 1938-2009), Redha Goubran (1945-1997), Ahmed Saad, Abdellaim Zaki (1939), and in another generation there was Shwekar Khalifa(1943) the first female animator.

After Mona Abu Alnasr came back from studying animation in California, she established her own studio, "Cairo Cartoon", and started her own projects in cooperation with Egyptian TV, which formalized the 1990s and 2000s as the golden age of Egyptian animation. Right now in Egypt there are about 50 animation studios, which vary in size and capacity. There are around ten big studios, which provide more than 100 animated hours yearly, including series, episodes, ads and short films.
"Al Sahar studio" was established by Ben Alabbas, the Saudi investor in the early 90s and tried to work on the first Egyptian feature animated film, The Knight and the Princess which is not yet finished due to lack of funds.

The work primarily is 2-D and clay animation, in addition to new studios that work with 3-D and Flash. Some studios, such as "Tarek Rashed", specialize in 3-D. "Zamzam" studio specializes in religious series produced in clay animation. There are medium-sized studios, such as "A+ Cartoon" and "Cartoonile", who use Flash techniques to produce for Egyptian TV.

In addition to the specialist studios, there are a lot of free-lancers who work individually or part-time, such as the award winners Hussain Nemr, Hazem Gooda, Ahmed Fathi and Mohamed Ghazala, who produced Honayn's Shoe, the winner of the Best Animation prize in African Movie Academy Awards - Nigeria 2010. In the educational aspect, every year there are more than 200 graduating BA students who studied animation for at least two years, and half of them continue working in animation as their career.

In Egypt, there are two international festivals that have animation categories in their competitions: Cairo International Cinema Festival for Children and Ismailia International Film Festival for Documentary and Short films. There are some local events, such as Al Sakia Animation festival, and the Society of Egyptian Animation Festival every February.

Mohamed Ghazala

Mohamed Ghazala,Ph.D, Assistant professor in Minia University- Director of ASIFA Egypt.

Workshop of Narcisse Youmbi in Cameroon

Heikki Jokinen with members of ASIFA Egypt in lecture in Bibliotheca Alexandrina

Frenkel Brothers
The first steps of animation in Egypt

الإخوان فرنكل
الخطوات الأولى للرسوم المتحركة في مصر

في الوقت الـذي كـان رائـد الرسوم المتحركـة العالمي، والـت ديزنـي Disney (١٩٠١-١٩٦٦) ينتج أول أفلامه الطويلة سنوويات والأقزام السبعة في أواخر الثلاثينيات من القرن العشرين، كـان هنـاك عائلـة صـغيرة تقيم في الإسكندرية، تسعى جاهدة لعمل فيلمهـا المتحرك الأول على نمط أفلام التحريك التي بدأت تصل إلى مصر من هوليوود لتعرض قبل العروض السينمائية الطويلة في دور العرض في القاهرة والإسكندرية.
كانت عائلة فرنكل تمتهن النجارة والطباعة منذ هجرتها الباكرة في مطلع القرن إلى مصر قادمين من روسيا، وقد كان أبناءها موهوبين بالفطرة ، فقد كانوا مغرمين بالأفلام الأمريكية وخاصة لشارلي تشابلن، كما كان أحدهم مهتماً بالرسم والتلوين، بينما الأخر كان حاذقاً في مجال الميكانيكا والأدوات والكهرباء.

كان شغفهم بمشاهدة السينما ملهماً لهم ليصنعوا أفلامهم الخاصة. فادخروا من ميزانيتهم الخاصة مـا يمكنهم من استثمار بعض المـال في صنع الأفلام، التي لم يكون يعرفون عن صناعتها شيئاً من قبل، فكان عليهم اختراع اختراع آلاتهم الخاصة بأنفسهم.
في البدأ اتفقوا على تصميم شخصية القرد مـاركو، وهو مـا كلفهم الكثير من الوقت والجهد لإنجاز عشر دقائق من التحريك الذي أستغرق رسمه تصميم أكثر من ١٥٠٠٠ رسمه بطول ١٦٠٠ متر من الفيلم الخام.
كان النتيجة مرضيه لهم أخيراً..فقد شاهدوا تحريكهم بأيديهم، وأشركوا جمهور شـارعهم بمشاهدة فيلمهم الأول.. وعلى الرغم من ترحاب الكثيرين بهذا السبق الفني، فقد انتقدتهم الصحف لتشابه شخصيات فيلمهم الأول "القرد ماركو" مع أبطال أفلام والـت ديزنـي.

بفضل حماسهم والتشجيع الذين لاقوه من جيرانهم عن فيلمهم الأول، كـان اندفاعهم لإنتاج فيلمهم التـالي الـذي تعثر من قلـة الدعم والموارد المالية المطلوبة لإنتاجه. وقد سعوا للحصول على العديد من الممولين و المساهمين ولكن بـلا فـائدة.. ويومـاً مـا قال لهم أحد الأثرياء :سوف أعطيكم المال في المشمش ! ..وعادوا ليخبروا والدهم "مـا فيش فايدة" ! ومن هنا كان اختيارهم لأسم شخصيتهم الجديدة: مشمش أفندي ، وأسم الفيلم "ما فيش فايدة" !
وكان على الأخوان فرنكل أن ينتجوا فيلمهم بالجهود الذاتية خلال عدة أعوام إلى أن انتهوا من تنفيذ الفيلم ليعرض أخيراً في الثامن من فبراير عام ١٩٣٦ بسينما كوزموجراف (حاليـاً سينما كوزموس بوسط القاهرة) وأستمر عرضه إلى عام ١٩٣٩ بنجاح مستمر يصحبه إشادة الإعلام. حيث يمكن وقتها مطالعة أحد عناوين جريدة "La Bourse Egyptienne" يقول : أخيراً أصبح لميكي ماوس شقيق مصري !

وبينما كانت الحرب العالمية الثانية في أوج عنفوانها تحتدم على بوابة مصر الغربية بقدوم النازيين لمقاتلة البريطانيين الذين مازالوا يملكون زمام الأمور في مصر بالرغم من سلطان الملك فاروق، فقد كلفت وزارة الدفاع المصرية في العام ١٩٣٩ الأخوان فرنكل لعمل فيلم للتعبئة ودعم و مساعدة الجيش المصري في أثناء الحرب. فأنتجوا فيلم "الدفاع الوطني" الـذي حمل فيه مشمش أفندي لواء الحملة الوطنية للتبرع للجيش. كما أنه قام باختراع أجهزة لتدمير العدو، وحمل مصر على الانتصار في النهاية.
تم العرض الأول للفيلم في مارس عام ١٩٤٠ بعد تجاوز الأخوة فرنكل الكثير من المصاعب والتحديات السياسية، ومحاولتهم التقريب مابين وجهات نظر الرقابة الوطنية والاحتلال البريطاني.

في السنين اللاحقة، أقدم الإخوان فرنكل على صنع العديد من الأفلام القصيرة والإعلانات التجارية من بينها أفلام قدموا فيها الدمج مابين الفيلم الحي والرسوم المتحركة كما فعلوا مع المطربة صباح وتحية كاريوكا الذين مثلوا مع شخصيتهم البطلة مشمش أفندي في مشاهد غنائية مرحة.

حتى العام ١٩٥١ كانت أجواء الثورة قد بدأت في الاتقاد، وكانت طوائف الأجانب المقيمين في مصر متخوفين من تلك الأجواء التي قد تعصف باستثماراتهم في مصر ومستقبلهم الاقتصادي. ففكر الأخوة فرنكل في الهجرة إلى فرنسا.
من الطريف أنه بالرغم من أن كل أفلام فرنكل المتحركة قد أنتجت جميعاً في مصر، وكتب على كل منها في المقدمة "إنتاج مصري"، فإن الجمارك المحلية اعتبرت تلك الأفلام "صناعة أجنبية"، نظراً لجنسية صانعيها، وعليه فقد تمكنوا من نقل أفلامهم بالكامل معهم وهم في طريقهم إلى أوروبا !

بالقرب من باريس، تحول قبو منزلهم إلى أستوديو سينمائي ليواصل الإخوة فرنكل حلمهم في الإنتاج السينمائي . ولكي يبدو مشمش أفندي ـشخصيتهم الأسطوريةـ أقرب لأن يكون فرنسياً، فقد استبدلوا طربوشه الأحمر بقبعة قصيرة ، كما غيروا اسم مشمش إلى ميميش Mimiche ليبدو أكثر باريسية!
وبذلك انطوت أولى صفحات تاريخ فن التحريك في مصر، ليبدأ جيل لاحق من المصريين مكملين مسيرة الإخوة فرنكل.

د. محمد غزالة

IHAB SHAKER
by Mohamed Ghazala

Ihab Shaker.

Giannalberto Bendazzi described Ihab Shaker, the painter of the 2011 ASIFA's poster for International Animation Day (IAD), as "the most famous animation film director beyond the borders of his homeland." Heba Elkayal, the Egyptian writer, noted, "His animation reveals an artist of versatile talents".

Shaker was born in Cairo, in 1933, received his first lesson in art, when he was still a boy, with an Italian professor, then joined the Leonardo Da Vinci School and, later, graduated from the faculty of Fine Arts in 1957. He started work in newspaper illustration in 1953. His work established him, while he was a young student, as a highly celebrated caricaturist for the Al-Gomhuria newspaper, and his career encompasses a well-known legacy of caricature.

He directed many animated films in Egypt beginning in 1968 and then moved to France, where he met and worked with the French pioneer Paul Grimault (Walt Disney's French and equally celebrated counterpart, as Shaker addressed in one of his interviews) who helped Shaker to direct his work entitled Un Deux Trois, which earned Shaker the prestigious Prix de Qualité (1973). Later, Shaker became the first Egyptian and African member of ASIFA. Then he returned home, though he would revisit France intermittently including a stint as a member of the jury in Annecy (1993).

Shaker feels that the thesis, which he edited as proposal to gain a grant from UNESCO, and submitted to the Canadian animation artist Norman McLaren in 1968, concerned the idea of music in art. "These were studies about movement in art. How you can employ time in manipulating the three dimensions. And my breakthrough would be the idea of music as architecture in motion." – from an interview in Al-Ahram weekly, 1999.

The Egyptian animator summed up in a newspaper interview: "Disney's ingenuity of animation was in expressing the movement in its best imagery. This which attracted me to the art of animation." Ihab Shaker followed, "I spent three years to study the movement of the horse steps to appear finally in my film The Dance of Love.... The motion comes from the psychical depth, which selects the feature of the shape and the expressed action. While in painting I face challenge to express it, animation gives me the tool to express these deep feelings".

Ihab Shaker and Paul Grimault in front of the Sphinx.

Still from Love Dance by Ihab Shaker.

Ihab Shaker with Raoul Servais and jury members to Cairo Children Cinema Festival 1992.

Animators in Finland do a pixilated film on International Animation Day. The films called Animation Revolution are screened later on that very day. Still from 2007, directed by Kaisa Penttilä.

Kaisa Penttilä: Animaation vallankumous, 2007

ASIFA FINLAND

ASIFA-Finland was established in May 2000 after ASIFA Nordic - covering all five Nordic countries and three Baltic countries - was terminated. Finns did not want to lose the link to ASIFA.

In practical terms, ASIFA-Finland work is merged together with the older national animation association, Animation Clinic. In a small country like Finland, there was no point establishing two organizations to do the same work.

`ASIFA-Finland's profile is most visible through the International Animation Day on 28th October. Every year, ASIFA-Finland joins this global event and prints a Finnish version of the international poster.

The global ASIFA network is also available to Finnish animators through ASIFA-Finland.

Other actions for animation take place under the auspices of Animation Clinic.

Heikki Jokinen

Heikki is ASIFA Vice-President and serves as a liaison between ASIFA and festivals.

Suomen Asifa perustettiin toukokuussa 2000 sen jälkeen kun kaikki Pohjolan ja Baltian maat kattanut Asifa Nordic lopetti toimintansa. Suomalaiset eivät halunneet menettää linkkiä Asifaan.

Käytännössä Suomen Asifan toiminta on sulautettu jo aiemmin toimineeseen Animaatioklinikkaan. Pienessä maassa ei ollut mielekästä perustaa uutta päällekkäistä järjestöä, jossa olisivat kuitenkin toimineet samat ihmiset.

Asifa-profiili näkyy selvimmin maailman animaatiopäivän

järjestämisessä 28. lokakuuta. Suomi on joka vuosi mukana maailmanlaajuisessa tapahtumassa ja painatamme kansainvälisen julisteen suomalaisen version. Muutoinkin pyrimme tarjoamaan Asifan kansainvälisen verkoston suomalaisille animaationtekijöille. Muu toiminta animaation hyväksi tapahtuu Animaatioklinikan kautta.

2008, the Hiroshima festival esented a major retrospective Finnish animation. The Finnish imators Sanna Vilmusenaho d Ami Lindholm together with na Kawamura from The Finnish mbassy in Japan at the festival.

Uralin Perhonen (Far from Ural, 2008) created a major discussion in Finland with it's fresh views of the national history.
Puppet animator Katariina Lillqvist is one of the best know Finnsh animation directors.

ASIFA FRANCE

Juliette Crochu.

Created in 1971, AFCA, French Animated Film Association, emerged out of a wide movement of recognition and promotion of animation in France that had started years earlier, lead by two passionate movie-goers, André Martin and Michel Boschet.

The first meetings about animation art, organized in Cannes in 1956 and 1958, spurred the idea of the need for founding a national association. In 1957, ACA, Association for Artists and Friends of Animated Film, was created, bringing together Alexandre Alexeïeff, Arcady, Berthold Bartosch, Omer Boucquey, Paul Grimault, Henri Gruel, Jean Image, and Raymond Maillet.

The creation of ASIFA, in 1960, would soon command greater energy and significance and lead the ACA to its decline in 1968. In 1971, at a time when many producers and national associations sprung up around the world, ASIFA-France was created to bring together all the professionals of the field in the country. Following a dispute over the organization's process, a split occurred within ASIFA, leading to the creation of AFCA.

Afca office.

Raymond Maillet was AFCA's general delegate from 1971 to 1993. He also managed the Annecy Festival from 1960 to 1981. In 1975, AFCA began publishing a newsletter along with the presentation of monthly screenings called "Animathèque."

In 1983, AFCA launched a national festival of animated films. Since the 1990's, new activities were developed such as the website, the publication of a guide for professionals, the International Animation Day celebration, a centre of research, and a shop.

In 2000, AFCA renewed contact with ASIFA by creating a "footbridge", AFCA-ASIFA-France, allowing the AFCA members to become members also of ASIFA.

AFCA still develops its activities through three key aspects: events, resources and publications. It is meant to be an observatory of contemporary production and creation which takes into account the new trends in the field of animation. AFCA is permanently involved in collecting and processing information which serves as an important resource for institutions and organizations.

AFCA currently encompasses a large range of members, including directors, producers, distributors, animation schools, cultural organizations and amateurs. AFCA also regularly cooperates with French institutions and festivals as well as abroad with about 40 countries.

Text by Afca-ASIFA-France

Bruz 2010 Lunchtime.

ASIFA GREECE

ASIFA-Greece was founded in 2008 and since then its aim has been to connect the Greek and international animation network, as well as to maintain the connection with the contemporary world of art and animation, and to provide information thereof.

ASIFA-Greece and its members share the obligation to serve the art of animation, a field they love, to do continue to help its growth and development. ASIFA-Greece plays a key role in negotiating better terms for animation employment and also promotes the art of animation to the wider public, with the aid of public or private organizations.

For the achievement of the aforementioned goals, public screenings of animation films and seminars are organized. Children's workshops have been also organized to introduce them to the art of animation, and perhaps encourage future creators and audiences.

Anastasia Dmitra

Frame from The Circle.

Frame from The Gravity.

Anastasia is from Greece, teaching as well designing animation. She is currently the president of ASIFA Workshops Group and is Treasurer of ASIFA.

Η ASIFA Ελλάδος ιδρύθηκε το 2008 με σκοπό την σύνδεση του ελληνικού με το διεθνή ιστό της κινούμενης εικόνας, καθώς και τη

διατήρηση της επαφής και της ενημέρωσης περί τα σύγχρονα δρώμενα του κόσμου της 8ης

Τέχνης.

Η ASIFA Ελλάδος και τα μέλη της, θεωρούν υποχρέωσή τους να υπηρετούν το

χώρο της κινούμενης εικόνας, ένα χώρο που αγαπούν και θέλουν να δουν να

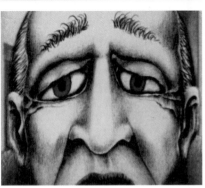

μεγαλώνει και να ASIFA Ελλάδος, μπορεί να κληθεί να παίξει έναν κύριο ρόλο όσον αφορά στην διεκδίκηση καλύτερων όρων εργασίας και να προωθήσει την τέχνη των

κινούμενων εικόνων στο ευρύ κοινό με τη βοήθεια κρατικών και μη φορέων.

Για την επίτευξη των παραπάνω στόχων διοργανώνονται προβολές ταινιών κινούμενων εικόνων, ημερίδες με θέμα την κινούμενη εικόνα, παιδικά εργαστήρια με

στόχο τη γνωριμία των παιδιών με την 8η Τέχνη, έτσι ώστε να γίνουν ένα θερμό μελλοντικό κοινό ή ακόμα καλύτερα οι αυριανοί δημιουργοί στο χώρο αυτό.

Τελευταία, η ASIFA Ελλάδος έχει θέσει υπό την αιγίδα της το φεστιβάλ της Σύρου

ANIMASYROS, ένα φεστιβάλ που στόχο έχει να προβάλλει την τέχνη του animation.

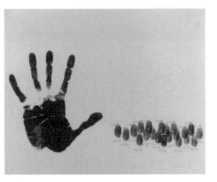

from top to bottom:
Frame from Cosmos,
Frame from The Village,
Frame from Odeur de Ville,
Frame from Walk,
Frame from The Line.

163

ASIFA INDIA

As ASIFA celebrates it's 50th anniversary, ASIFA-India celebrates it's 10th anniversary. The India chapter was founded in 2000 by Bill Dennis. The office was initially located in Thiruvananthrapurum (Trivandrum), in the South of India. There were only ten members. Today, the office is located in Mumbai (Bombay) with over 50 international members. ASIFA-India coordinates activities in 13 cities around the country. In 2010, ASIFA-India opened three subchapters in Indore, Pune and Hyderabad. The Mumbai office will remain the central location of ASIFA and will continue to plan and execute activities throughout the country. ASIFA-India is particularly proud of the activities planned for Indian artists and animators. Last year, during International Animation Day, nearly 15,000 attended the event in 13 different cities. The celebration included film competition, workshops, film screenings and demonstrations. Throughout the year, many international guest speakers conducted forums on leading edge technology and creative advances. ASIFA-India is led by Sarawati Balgam (Vani) who is assisted by Prasad and Amit. Bill Dennis continues to serve as President Emeritus. The offices are in the Rhythm & Hues Studios in Mumbai.

ASIFA-India does not charge a chapter membership fee. All events are open to the general public. It survives off of contributions from a handful of corporate supporters.

Everyone at ASIFA-India sends its congratulations to ASIFA on its 50th Anniversary.

Bill Dennis

Bill Dennis is founder of ASIFA-India and ex-Executive Director of ASIFA.

IAD Celebration pictures with ASIFA India.

OMID RAWHANI
Interview with Noureddin Zarrinkelk

Watching all the animation movies made by the American studios like Pixar and Walt Disney, or the new examples of Japanese animation such as Miyazaki, it seems that the situation of the animation market is very good. But as your information and knowledge about this subject is more complete and more accurate, and as you're also familiar with animations from countries like Czech Republic, Hungary, and the countries formerly known as Yugoslavia - which used to be the best during the 60's and 70's -- I'd like to ask you to draw an overall vision of today's global state of this art. Please give us more details about the current space of the animation in the world.

Would you think that still there are two distinct types of audiences: the general public and the elites?
It is an indisputable fact that we've moved from an era into another. What you do remember from decades of 60 and 70 was a specific kind of animation that today does not exist anymore. We've crossed that period to enter a new one.

Let's review the past for a better understanding of the present. Yes, we had two gold decades in the history of animation especially in the eastern European countries, as you mentioned. Those were also the decades of the Cold War between East and West, but this growth in the art of animation was not necessarily the result of the Cold War period but it was something that happened in parallel.

I belong to that era. I learned the necessary skills to make animation, like many of my colleagues of the same generation, during those years. We took advantage of the numerous opportunities offered to us. We participated in many festivals in the East and West, and we proved to the world that we could make films. At a time when travel to the eastern countries was prohibited, we freely travelled to the countries behind the iron wall, and it was a blessing to go and see something that so many were deprived of including the traditional filmmakers!

But after the collapse of the East block and the failure of the communism, the structure and shape of the animated films totally changed.

And what happened to creative animators, painters and designers? Most of them were hired by western studios or migrated to other countries where they were needed. Many of them were absorbed in Canadian or American markets and joined western commercial animation industry and markets. This way the "See-saw" balance between two sides of iron curtain broke down.....

And how did it help to the growth of this movement; From the artistic point of view and from the quality of drawing and designing?
I am afraid that the creative animation with classic definitions disappeared, or at least got out of that effective trend,. But this phenomena was the result of the introduction of computers into the world of animation, first in the western countries and then even into the East. The computerized animation changed everything; it facilitated the difficulties of traditional animation making and added new dimensions to it.

It was how small rooms or home "garages" replaced big studios, and less experienced but interested youngsters joined this trend and became expert in it. Some of them vanished from the competition, however those who remained, joined to the animation family.
And they replaced the traditional animator positions. Right?
Yes, many talented and genius artists among them popped up who completely changed the cinema's direction. The old world changed into a new world; the world of 60's and 70's joined the history and a new era replaced the venue of animation.

Moreover, we are once again about to witness the transformation of an era into the other.   I think that the future of animation is far beyond the place it is right now. This is a turning point. I'd even say that the animation will replace live action Hollywood cinema! Soon there will be no more live action movie directors but someone who knows animation or have an animator co-director.
Like Avatar?
Avatar is a live movie; but it is based on animation techniques and structures. In fact, Hollywood is a live film factory; but having the animation technology in which live action becoming a part of it....

Like "Alice in wonderland by "Tim Burton".......
Yes, these kinds of artists are giant animators; however, bigger animators will come up and transform the cinema. The production of movies would be much easier and less expensive due to the increasing use of animation technologies and more powerful computers to generate the most expensive scenes and scenarios. The technology of animation will develop where no visual tricks is needed, no permanent presence of actors or actresses, no expensive and busy locations anymore. Methods of computer production and animation works will do all the tasks.

And these so-called contemporary live action/animations like "transformers" Avatar and Alice and other are initiation of forthcoming transformations.

If you ask me what would be the entire conclusion, in fact, I cannot consider an end to it. We are in 21th century. We are at the beginning of a quick evolution of technologies, in comparison, like Jules Verne whose imagination was not believed to come true during his own time. What he predicted and wrote was his imagination and it came true after almost 1- 2 centuries. But at the moment, we are in a Jules Verne-like-period, but in our case, it would takes only one decade or two for an idea/ imagination to actually become reality!

One of the events which affected the current situation –like the role of MTV clips in development and improvement of cinema and technical structure of live action movies - were computer games, a new venue which opened the doors for imagination.
Did the production and the success of these computer games affect and transform the animation world?

I call these computer games the children of animation. Eventually, they became more developed than their mother! These games are growing in the matrix of computer and born from them. The trend of their evolution is parallel with the progress of animation technologies. We're not so much far from live action movies. The continuation of this transformation is the same as what we talked earlier, about becoming needlessness from live action filmmaking! Tragic and painful, isn't it?
Going back to the first question, what happened to the creative animators from countries like Czech Republic, Poland, Yugoslavia....
The fall of the Iron Curtain, the collapse of the Soviet Union had fine

consequences for their people: Freedom, Welfare, and getting rid of dictators etc .....; however it had negative aspects as well.

One of the negative consequences was to disappear their significant animation, or their national cinema in one word.

After breaking down of East block and the apparition of different political flows in these countries, it seems that animation vanished and since then, the thoughtful and balanced production has disappeared. Both productive studios and independent productions got sold out. A generation has been exterminated. From the dinosaurs of those era only a few remain who are in hospitals waiting for angel of death, like Kawamoto the famous Japanese director who died just when we were interviewing, or rare lucky ones who may spend their time with their grand children in the parks.

I was in one of the main animation festivals recently. You will be surprised if I tell you that there were no more than a few good movies (57 film out of 1975 film)! While parallel with it there were galleries/show rooms full of old artistic films, wisdom and humanistic messages .....what a contrast!!

In the old times, in the festivals (such as festival for children and young adults in Tehran) we used to see at least 10-20 great films. But here were many experimental films made just for winning rewards; but empty of any touching sense or acceptable message. This is becoming a trend in our age. Nothing else but Just to "product" more with no quality! And it happens when our world is full of oppression, poverty, violence, terrorism and genocide which all are the dark side of human race.

These large number of movie production; how can be judged fairly? The high number of movies makes it very hard for the judgment too! The selection committee has to watch 2000 films in 15 days or so! And as they don't have enough time, they have to see 2-3 minutes of a movie and put it away!

While there may be some films that you don't get their messages unless you see the last minute or even the last frame. Thus, it would be necessary to change the system of selection in order to NOT forego quality for quantity. I am writing an article on this subject where I will suggest a new system of selection. It may be in this book or in the Asifa Magazine. And I hope to hear from my other colleagues' reasonable solutions as well.

ASIFA
IRAN

ASIFA IRAN

Iranian animation has seen three different periods in its half a century history: Birth, early 1960s to the 1980s; Winter sleep, from 1980s to mid-90s; Rebirth, since mid-90s.

At the end of the 1950s, when Mr. E. Ahmadieh was a young boy, he noticed the illusion of movement in animation while looking at the consecutive frames of a cartoon on celluloid. He was so excited about his discovery that he decided to experience it himself. Using a 16 mm Bolex camera, he succeeded in finding a way to animate his drawings. This was how the animation was re-invented in Iran, after its original invention by Emil Kohl more than 5 decades earlier!

During this same period, another young artist, N. Karimi, who had studied cinema and animation in Prague, and later, caricaturist J. Tejaratchi joined them. These three animators made the first animation studio in Iran at the Iranian bureau for Art &Culture and together they created the very first animated short film.

The real movement in creative animation began after 1966 when an important international animation festival for children and youth was launched in Tehran. There were many brilliant films made by artists such as Norman McLaren, Raoul Servais, Bordo Dovnikovic, Frederick Back, Fyodor Khitruk, John and Faith Hubley, Bruno Bozzetto, Břetislav Pojar and many other great artists from Eastern European and Western countries. This allowed Iran to open a panoramic vision of quality animation to young and eager talents inside the country who had no access to such advanced art at the time.

Due to the success of this festival, a new wave of demand for high quality animation emerged among both the cultural authorities and inspiring artists in Iran. A colorful spectrum of educated designers, illustrators, graphic designers and painters, such as F. Mesghali, A. A. Sadeghi, N. Riyahi, M. Momayez were attracted to the art of animation, which could give movement and speech to their static forms of arts and make their works much more attractive.

The Center for Development of Children and Young Adults- "KANOON"- which was the first and largest (on the world scale) artistic and cultural organization for young adults, opened studios, invited talented artists, and produced experimental and professional animated shorts. This institute was founded and managed by Lily Arjomand and Firouz Shirvanlou in late 1950's to cover all cultural needs of children to include libraries, showrooms, workshops, books, etc. and all art forms created for and by them.

As soon as an educated animator, Noureddin Zarrin-Kelk came back from Belgium, having studied animation at Raoul Servais's animation department in Royal Academy of Fine Arts in Ghent (1969 - 1971), he founded the first animation school in Iran for the pre-college level for KANOON 1974 then three years later, at the University of Arts, Farabi. These students either formed assistant teams for pioneers or worked as independent animators. They are now masters and professors of animation both inside and outside Iran, at Walt Disney and other major studios. In less than a decade (1970-78) dozens of high quality animated films were produced in KANOON that achieved high international recognition and awarded international prizes from festivals world over.

After this strong beginning, animation went into hibernation due to the Iran-Iraq war and the cultural revolution. Animators, as well as other artists, either changed careers, or sought jobs or business outside of Iran. During this period, the only school of animation at the Farabi University and the rest of the Universities and Art schools closed along with the International Festival for Children and Youth.

Consequently, the production of animation almost died. It was considered non-Islamic. On the flip side a few things happened to ensure animation did not completely die. KANOON (which was reorganized on Islamic bases) put some effort into keeping animation alive. It produced several short animated films by the second generation of animators such as M Javaherian,   V. F. Moghadam, A.

Photos from top to bottom:
V.F.Moghadam, M.Khoramiyan,
R.Sadeghi, M.Javaherian.

Alimorad, and R.N. Azadani, A. Arabani, A .Asghar-zadeh, F. Torabi plus few beginners in the field. A new animation school began working inside the radio & television organization under S. Tavakolian. An Islamic based training university was founded to teach animation courses, at Master's level managed by A. Alami and taught by a Russian professor. In parallel with the fading out of the older artists and art schools, new non-artistic organizations such as religious art schools, were opened to educate and produce films, including animated ones.

In rebirth a number of initiatives allowed animation to come back to life in Iran. Computers arrived to private homes and encouraged young people to create primitive movements, and make simple animated stories. Saba, a TV organization, was founded with a mission statement to produce and sponsor animated Iranian TV series according to the Cultural Revolution's guidelines based on Islamic patterns. Social reforms (1997-2005) opened supporting attitude to the art forms, including animation. Hundreds of studios started up since then and produced thousands of minutes of TV animated series for children and educative purposes. Due to the increase in population, the need of animation grew and the budgets for animation increased, though not as much. An international biennial festival of animated films was launched by KANOON in 2000. Quite a few private animation courses and schools were started and added to the three existing main animation schools from which hundreds of students have since been trained. Also, The Center for Promoting Documentary, Short Films was founded by Ministry of Culture and Islamic Guidance to support young filmmakers and animators who created a new genre of animated films.

Regardless of the huge economic inflation and low income, animation is still quite attractive to new generations of the middle and low class. Many animators still run their studios under difficult conditions and some artists build their careers by getting income through other arts such as graphic, illustration, etc. This way animation is surviving.

Photos from top to bottom:
S.Tavakolian, Razani,
N.Yaghmaian, M.Azizi.

During the last decade six/seven feature animated films and a few games have been produced with a more under production by both government organizations and the private sector. Altogether, some 1800 names appear in "The Comprehensive Book of Animation of Iran, 2008-2009" among which are dozens of talented artists that are the backbone of the new commercial and TV serial productions. You may follow the entire list of the names and their careers at the following sites: http://www.idba.ir, http://www.kanoonnews.ir, http://hozehonari.com, and http://sabaanima.com.

ASIFA Iran, the oldest Iranian artistic association, was unofficially born in 1978 by its founder, Noureddin ZarrinKelk. In the beginning, it faced the revolution, so its meetings were held at the member's homes as a shared need and interest. Since 1986, when the association went public, the number of members soared from 12 to 350 today. Its programs include meetings, shows, seminars, ceremonies and international animation day activities.

ASIFA-Iran joined ASIFA in the 1990's and in 1995 was merged with the syndicated organization House of Cinema of Iran. ASIFA-Iran is reorganized as the main non-profit, non-political animation organization in Iran, supporting any progressive movement in animation. The present board of directors of ASIFA-Iran is composed of: N. ZarrinKelk (president, entitled father of Iranian animation), R. Sadeghi (Ed), K.Darvishi (Webmaster), E. Sharie(treasurer), and A. Arabani (Editor of Asifa-Iran's magazine).

Noureddin ZarrinKelk

Noureddin is founder of ASIFA-Iran and an ex-ASIFA President.

Three generations of Iranian animators
at new year ASIFA meeting in 2007:
From left: B.Gharibpour, M.Azizi,
N.Nima, A.Arabani, E.Ahmadieh,
N.Zarrin Kelk, N.Karimi, H.khorzuqi,
K.DarvishiN.Rabet, V.F.Moghadam
National members are 600 and
Intl. members are 80 now.

من واسفا

سال ۱۹۶۹ من دانشجوی انجمن در شهرگنت (گان) بلژیک بودم دفتم کرته
«وظیفه، اول» را دنستم می ختم که دراول سروده ستا دم علام کرد مرکز فیلس
شهرست می آمراه آزمای فستیوال آنسی فرانسه لقرتند.
اولین حضور درجشنواره ای درآن سری وطن تجربه تازه ای بودم برای من تازه کاری
خارج ازدنیای روزانه زندگی است وللذوتی دیگر دارد.
به مرزور دهنری بود وبا همه ناشی گری کردرکار داشتم ، پا طمان بک مویلای
قدمی ودستگاه ضبط صوت مدرسه صداگذاری (افلت ومزک) را ب ها
داریم وماه می ۱۹۷۰ رفتیم که تا شهرگان ش دهزار کیلومتری ناصله دار
داز قضا- برنده دوم جائزه فستیوال بهم شدیم که یک فانوس کوچک بود .
در همین فستیوال بود کربا دیدار ارلیک آشنا شدم و او دروازه ای شک نامن
آزان به آسفیا را بیداشم . دیدار ارلیک مخترع هلوگرافی درانجمن بود ودهان
قدر کرمن برای او همراه داشتم ادیب همن هرداشت . (بعدا که مبتر نشتیم
فهمیدیم که همین مهرورزی را او دست به همه اقوام وملل او ا دم ع داشت
(زهندی وچمنی دسخول تا من که دولین ایرانی سرراه او بودم)
دیدم ازاسفیا گفت ومن ندانستم ازکی عضو انجمن بلما زان جهان (آسفیا)
شدام دا نیذه ایران درانسازمان ! (زیرا او ناینذه امریکا دراسفیا
عضو فعال و "وایس پریزیذنت" ان انجمن بود.)
آزان به بعد مرتبا محله آسفیا وناه های پریزنت اسفیا (جنایالاس)
را دریافت می کردم .

174

وقتی به ایران برگشتم و درجهت بازسازی استودیوی انیمیشن کانون پرورش و نیروی زمینی ارتش شتاب می بردم (قبلاً صاحب من درگذشته و من سرگرد ارتش و دکتر داروساز بهداری آن بودم) عاقبت حکم انتقال من به کانون صادر شد و در کانون مشغول کار شدم. قضارا میزبان لقمه رباحی هم که در ملک من در استودیوی تن تن کار را انیمیشن می کرد به ایران برگشته و در کانون پیوسته بود و او هم عضو آسیفا بود! پس آسیفا در ایران تنها نبود. بلکه دو عضو داشت. شش سال بعد وقتی دانشکدهٔ انیمیشن را در دانشگاه هنر رابی تأسیس کردم و تعداد دانشجویان به چهارده نفر رسید – درست در فرصتی و این باری ی طوفانی انقلاب – آسیفای ایران را با شرکت دانشجویان به طور غیر رسمی راه اندازی کردم در رسالت شدم عضو انجمن بین المللی آسیفا و چون دانشگاه ۴ تعطیل در ارکان ۴ وزارت خانه ی دولتی به هم ریختند به ناچار جلسات نمایش فیلم و کار های انجمنی مان را در خانهٔ اعضا تشکیل می دادیم. هر بار در خانهٔ یک عضو. دههٔ ۸۰ میلادی که هنوز اوضاع کشور انقلابی بود و جنگی را که صدام حسین دیوانهٔ قدرت برکشور و ملت ها تحمیل کرده با سامانی ۴ را تشدید کرده بود، آسیفا حیاتش را ادامه داد و در دورهٔ اصلاحات در هر که آسیفای ایران در صحنهٔ هنری ملی ظاهر بود و دارای اعضای بین المللی نشد. اسنادیاً ان نشر و عضو گیری شروع شد و پس در سال ۱۹۹۵ به عضویت "خانهٔ سینما" در آمد که خود تازه اعلام موجودیت کرده بود و فعالیتهای سینمائی کشور را نزدیک بهتر می طلبید. برساس مقررات آسیفا، موظف بودم هر سال جدا تشکیل کنم برای

مجلس هست مدیرهٔ آسفای بین الملل که ۲۲ نفر بود شرکت کنم تا این که در سال ۲۰۰۳ به پیشنهاد دیوید اریک و رأی ۴۳ عضو هیئت مدیرهٔ آسفا عهده دار ریاست این انجمن شدم و سه سال احکام وظیفه کردم. پیش از من برژس کی لاران (کانادا) جان ۴ لاک ۳ (بریتانیا) پال و سرده ۳ (بلژیک)، میشل اسیلو (فرانسه)، آبی فی هو ۵ (پرتقال) توماس رونازور ۶ (اتریش) ... و بعد از من سایمو کو کنزو شیا ۷ (ژاپن) دلرون شین ۸ دکره) رئیس جمهور آسفا شدند.

(اگر کسی را جا انداخته ام لطفاً اصلاح کند) صالح
انجمن آسفا را آنیا که من شناخته ام می توانم انجمن خورشنام گردون آگروی ۹ سیاسی، مالی و حرفه رائی ی شخصی معرفی کنم در آن افتخار کنم.

نورالدین زرین کلک
۸ شهریور ۱۳۸۹

NOUREDDIN ZARRINKELK

ASIFA and I

In 1969, when I was in the middle of making Duty, first - my first film as a student of animation in Ghent, Belgium -- my teacher Raoul Servais let us know which student was allowed to send his/her finished movie to the Annecy Festival.

Of course, you can imagine how much this promise - attending this international festival -- for a novice like me with little experience in animation was sweet and appealing, like a dream come true.

So I did my best to finish my movie, using an old editing desk and our school's tape recorder for effect and music. Finally, in May 1970, I drove to the festival (some 1000 kilometers distance from Ghent) and luckily, our school ended up receiving the prize: a hand-made lantern!

Clip from Bani Adam 2010.

The other great outcome of being at the Annecy Festival was to meet David Ehrlich for the first time, and he became the one who gave me the chance of being part of ASIFA. David Ehrlich was the inventor of holography in animation; but the main reason that I had lots of respect for him was his love towards people. Actually, when I got to know him better, I found out that David, by nature, treated any race and nationality with the same kindness, no matter where they came from.

Through him, I got involved with ASIFA and before I knew I became the representative of Iran at the organization! David himself was an active member of ASIFA-East and a vice president of ASIFA-International at the time.

It was how I started receiving regularly the ASIFA's magazines and the letters from the president of ASIFA.

After my return to Iran, I expressed my interest in joining Kanoon, "The Institute for Intellectual Development of Children and Young Adults"; But as I was still a Major/Doctor in Iranian Army, I became the object of a dispute between the Army and Kanoon which fortunately ended by my final transfer to Kanoon.

I started to make animated films and writing and illustrating books for children as soon as I got out of the army. Two years later I founded the first animation school in Iran (and near east) at college level from which 12 animators were trained.

Another three years later, I managed to open the Animation department in the Farabi University at MA level and taught 14 students. By now, Iran had become the official member of ASIFA-International with ten animation students and teachers.

Due to the 1979 uprising, and the cultural cleansing of the universities, Farabi Art University got closed in the middle of courses. So we decided to hold (unofficially) each of our meetings/screenings at an ASIFA member's home.

In the 80s, and during the years of the war with Iraq – a war imposed by the savage Saddam Hussein to our nation -- in spite of the difficult situation at every level in the country, ASIFA-Iran continued its activities.

During the rise of the reformists, new members joined ASIFA-Iran. A manifesto was written. Now ASIFA-Iran has 600 members, a new branch in Isfahan and around 30 international members.

In 1995, ASIFA-Iran became part of the "House of Cinema" which is the Iranian Alliance of Motion Picture Guilds which covers the whole country's cinema-related activities.

As one of the 22 members of ASIFA-International's board of directors, I had to participate in its annual meetings. Later in 2003, per David Ehrlich's suggestion and 36 board members' votes, I became president of ASIFA-International.

Norman McLaren, Jon Halas, Raoul Servais, Michel Ocelot, Abi Feijo, Thomas Renoldner had held the same title before me and I served ASIFA in this position for 3 years (2003-2006). At the end of this period, Sayoko Kinoshita and Nelson Shin became ASIFA-International's presidents.

ASIFA is a well known nonprofit organization with a very good name and with no political or commercial affiliation. I am very proud of my work and involvement in this NGO.

David Ehrlich, Eduard Nazarov and Noureddin ZarrinKelk at Annecy.

ASIFA ISRAEL

Top: Frome from Mermaid S.O.S. 2004. Dir Tsvika Oren and Avi Ofer. Above: Frome from Mom by Tal Barli.

Establishing ASIFA-Israel was initiated by producer-director-animator David 'dudu' Shalita, animator-lecturer -journalist Tsvi 'tsvika' Oren and director-designer Isaac Yoresh.

ASIFA Israel was officially established on April 2nd, 1985, with 27 active members and 14 correspondent members. Yoresh, head of Bezalel Academy's animation unit at the time, was elected chairman. Gil Alkabetz and Hanan Kaminsky were elected as board members. Offices were located at Bezalel, Jerusalem. In July 1985, ASIFA-Israel was approved by ASIFA's international board as a recognized national branch.

ASIFA-Israel's activities have included: issuing 9 to 12 news bulletins a year; initiated cooperation with important bodies such as the Tel Aviv Cinematheque, the Haifa International Film Festival, the Caricature & Comics Museum – Holon, the British Council and the Goethe Institut – Tel Aviv; organizing monthly events: screenings, exhibitions, workshops and lectures. Many of these events featured top local and international artists such as Jan Svankmajer, Yuri Norstein, Joanna Quinn, Bob Godfrey, Gil Alkabetz, Yuval Nathan, Jonathan Hodgson, Phil Mulloy and Michaela Pavlatova, to name but a few.

The main event organized by ASIFA-Israel is ASIF (the Hebrew word for Harvest), now an 12 year old tradition. It is the annual competitive mini-festival screening of Israel's independent, commissioned and student films.

ASIFA-Israel's logo was designed and animated by animation-illustration-photography artist Avi Ofer.

ASIFA-Israel's chairpersons over the years have included: Yoresh 1985 – 1991. Tsvika Oren 1991 – 1995. 2000. 2006. 2007. (coordinator 2010) 2011. Tal Barli 1996- 1997. Noam Meshulam 1998. Lea Berkovicz 1999. Ruth Yoel 2001. Tal Lotan. 2002 – 2004. Ohad Efrat. 2005. Gilat Parag. 2008 – 2009.
Contact – asifa.israel@gmail.com

Tsvika Oren

Tsvika is a veteran animator/director, journalist, festival adviser/curator and lecturer, he also co-established Asifa Israel and is currently its president.

Peter Baynton master-class at Haifa Int'l Film Festival 2010. An Asifa Israel event organized by the British Council and the Haifa Film Festival.

אסיפ"א ישראל.

היוזמה להקמת אסיפ"א ישראל באה מן הבמאי/מעצב יצחק יורש, האנימטור/מרצה/עיתונאי צביקה אורן והמפיק/במאי/אנימטור דודו שליטא. אסיפ"א ישראל נוסד רשמית בתאריך 2.4.85 עם 27 חברים ועוד 14 מכותבים. יורש, ראש היחידה לאנימציה בבצלאל דאז, נבחר כיו"ר. גיל אלקבץ וחנן קמינסקי נבחרו כחברי ועד. המשרד התארח בבצלאל, ירושלים. ביולי 1985 אישר ועד אסיפ"א בינ"ל את סניף ישראל של האיגוד.

במשך מרבית שנות פעילותו פירסם אסיפ"א ישראל 9 עד 12 ידיעונים בשנה, יזם שיתופי פעולה עם גופים חשובים כמוזיאון ישראל, מוזיאון ת"א, סינמטק ת"א, פסטיבל הקולנוע חיפה, המוזיאון לקריקטורה וקומיקס – חולון, הבריטיש קאונסיל ומכון גיתה – ת"א. עם אלה ועם נוספים ארגנו אירועים חודשיים: הקרנות, תערוכות, סדנאות והרצאות. רבים מן האירועים אירחו את טובי אמני האנימציה בארץ ובעולם. אם להזכיר מעטים מביניהם: יאן שואנקמאייר, יורי נורשטיין, ג'ואנה קווין, בוב גודפרי, גיל אלקבץ, יובל נתן, ג'ונתן הודג'סון, פיל מאלוי ומיכאלה פבלטובה.

האירוע העקרי המאורגן ע"י אסיפ"א ישראל הוא "אסיף", שהפך כבר למסורת ב- 12 שנות קיומו. אלו הקרנות הסיכום השנתיות של היצירה העצמאית, המסחרית והסטודנטיאלית באנימציה ישראלית. מיני-פסטיבל תחרותי של סרטים נבחרים המעניק פרסים כספיים ותעודות הוקרה. יושבי הראש של אסיפ"א ישראל: יורש 1985 – 1991. צביקה אורן 1991 – 1995. 2000. 2006. 2007. (מתאם פעיליות 2010). טל ברלי 1996 – 1997. נועם משולם 1998. לאה ברקוביץ' 1999. רות יואל 2001. טל לוטן 2002 – 2004. אוהד אפרת 2005. גילת פרג 2008 – 2009.
קשר: asifa.israel@gmail.com (אורן) רח' פרוג 22, ת"א 63417.
עיצוב ואנימציית לוגו: אמן האנימציה, האיור והצילום אבי עופר.

ASIFA's 50th Anniversary stamps issued in Israel.

Still from Meorot.

Get The Picture. 2009. Avi Ofer.

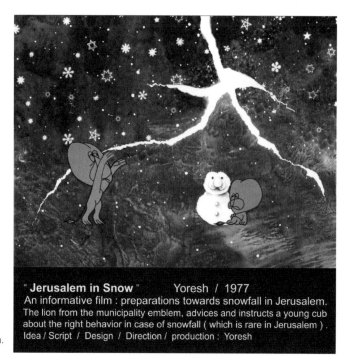

" **Jerusalem in Snow** " Yoresh / 1977
An informative film : preparations towards snowfall in Jerusalem.
The lion from the municipality emblem, advices and instructs a young cub
about the right behavior in case of snowfall (which is rare in Jerusalem).
Idea / Script / Design / Direction / production : Yoresh

Jerusalem in Snow by Yoresh.

ASIFAitalia
Associazione Italiana
Film d'Animazione
Archivio Storico del Cinema
d'Animazione Italiano

ASIFA ITALY

It is an old story, dating back in the early 1980's. During this time, the Italian animation cinema was in crisis. The landscape was desolated: producers were sparse and the filmmakers were lonely riders facing, on one hand, the cultural indifference of people towards cartoons and, on the other hand, the difficulties to gather different professionals to make up stable working teams.

In 1982 a small group of authors and artists decided to found, in Turin, the association ASIFA-Italia with two ambitious and long term aims; first, to promote the diffusion of animation cinema in Italy in order to make people more aware of the cultural value of this kind of art; second, to encourage helpful connections among animators, producers and screenwriters in order to coordinate their efforts to create working opportunities.

AMALFI, Cartoons on the Bay

In less than ten years of activity, ASIFA-Italia grew up and started to see its aims come to fruition. The organization gained the trust of authors and producers, becoming a landmark professionally and culturally. Since the mid-1990s, Italian production obtained new life blood, the studios increased in quality and quantity, rising from an artistic level to an industrial one, capable to deal with the new challenges of the market. The rise of animation companies in Italy led ASIFA-Italia to support the establishment of an association of firms (CARTOON ITALIA).

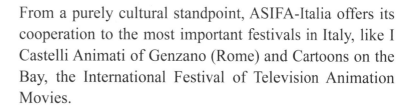

From a purely cultural standpoint, ASIFA-Italia offers its cooperation to the most important festivals in Italy, like I Castelli Animati of Genzano (Rome) and Cartoons on the Bay, the International Festival of Television Animation Movies.

ASIFA-Italia has also collected one the widest collection of documents on animation cinema in Europe, including a vast video and book library (more than 700 volumes), original drawings, and backgrounds, etc... Through its programs and the resources of its archive, the association organizes and participates in many festivals, meetings, seminaries, reviews, exhibitions, laboratories and lessons. In 2012, ASIFA-Italia will be 30 years old. Looking back we can see the footprints of those who decided to undertake a long journey devoted to the guardianship and promotion of the animation culture.

Text by ASIFA-Italy.

from top to bottom:
Osvaldo Cavandoli,
Guido Manuli,
Fusako Yusaki,
Bruno Bozzetto.

Poshano   Cartoons On the Bay.

ASIFA JAPAN

On December 22nd, 1981, under the initiative of Renzo Kinoshita, who was already an ASIFA Board Member at that time, a resolution was taken to establish ASIFA-Japan, at a meeting held at nac Image Technology Inc., in Tokyo. At that time, there were 22 ASIFA individual members in Japan, and among those, 15 members gathered at this meeting, including Taiji Yabushita, Yoji Kuri, Kihachiro Kawamoto, Osamu Tezuka, Edouard Herscovitz, etc. Also, Renzo Kinoshita was elected as the first President of ASIFA-Japan.

On December 22nd, 1982, the second General Assembly was held at the International House of Japan in Tokyo. We were very pleased to welcome June Foray as an important guest from ASIFA-Hollywood. She kindly talked about the Olympiad of Animation to be held in Los Angeles in 1984, and showed us several films from ASIFA-Hollywood.

On February 13th, 1984, the third General Assembly was held at the International House of Japan in Tokyo. I reported that Hiroshima City was considering the possibility of organizing an international animation festival under the Rules of ASIFA Patronized Competitive Festival, and that they would be making the decision by April 1984.

On April 12th, 1984, the Hiroshima City Council decided to co-organize an international animation festival together with ASIFA-Japan. It was decided that Renzo Kinoshita would serve as the Festival Producer, and I would be the Festival Director. The official logo of ASIFA-Japan was designed by Taku Furukawa. The First International Animation Festival in Japan – HIROSHIMA '85 was held from August 18th to 23rd, welcoming Paul Grimault, one of the ASIFA founders, as the Honorary President.

ASIFA-Japan holds a General Assembly annually, and re-elects a new Executive Board every three years. We have been working actively and voluntarily, ceaselessly for 30 years, in order to enhance the quality of Hiroshima Festival and to develop the art of animation through international exchange. At each Hiroshima Festival, we always hold an ASIFA Party, and organize the ASIFA Booth, in order to make funds for ASIFA's activity.

Since 1997, I have been serving as the President. I have also produced the exchange DVDs "ASIFA-JAPAN Vol. 1" and "Vol. 2".

During HIROSHIMA 2010, we were pleased to celebrate two anniversaries --- the 25th anniversary of Hiroshima Festival and the 50th anniversary of ASIFA ---, welcoming Raoul Servais as the Honorary President of ASIFA 50th Anniversary.

From left: Renzo Kinoshita, Yoji Kuri, Ishu Patel, unidentified at Yoji's studio

From left: Renzo Kinoshita, June Foray, Bill Scott, Sayoko Kinoshita.

Today, we are a branch of 62 members.

Sayoko Kinoshita

Sayoko is an award winning animation filmmaker/producer. With Renzo Kinoshita, she established the Hiroshima Int'l Animation Festival in 1985, and has been serving as the Festival Director since then. ASIFA Vice-President, ASIFA-Japan President, Visiting Professor at Osaka University of Arts.

Top: Illustration of Te Wei and Yan Ding Xian by Renzo Kinoshita 1981.
Bottom left: ASIFA Workshop Group screening participants.
Bottom right: Mayajima island.

ASIFA 日本支部

1981 年 12 月 22 日、（株）ナックの会議室にて、当時 ASIFA 理事であった木下蓮三のイニシアティヴにより、ASIFA 日本支部設立の決議がなされた。当時、日本には、22 名の ASIFA 個人会員がおり、その内、薮下泰次、久里洋二、川本喜八郎、手塚治虫、エド・ヘルスコヴィッチ等 15 名が決議に参加した。また、木下蓮三が、ASIFA-Japan 初代会長に選出された。
1982 年 12 月 22 日、第 2 回定期総会を国際文化会館にて開催。ASIFA-Hollywood から、ジューン・フォレイ女史をゲストとしてお迎えし、ロサンゼルスで 1984 年に開かれる『オリンピアード・オブ・アニメーション』について話して頂くと共に、ASIFA-Hollywood からの作品も上映して頂く。
1984 年 2 月 13 日、第 3 回定期総会を国際文化会館にて開催。木下小夜子は、広島市が ASIFA 公認規約に則った国際映画祭の開催を前向きに検討中であり、4 月中には結論が出る予定、と発表。役員改選が行なわれ、木下蓮三が会長に再選。1984 年 4 月 12 日、広島市議会は、ASIFA 日本支部との共催で国際映画祭を開催することを決定。木下蓮三がフェスティバルプロデューサーに、木下小夜子がフェスティバルディレクターに就任。
古川タクのデザインによる ASIFA 日本支部のロゴ決定。
1985 年 8 月 18 日～23 日、第 1 回国際アニメーションフェスティバル HIROSHIMA'85 開催。ASIFA 創設者の一人であるポール・グリモー氏を国際名誉会長に迎える。
以後、ASIFA 日本支部は、毎年の定期総会と 3 年に一度の役員改選を行ない、今日まで 30 年間、広島国際アニメーションフェスティバルの芸術的質の保持、運営、そして国際交流を通したアニメーション芸術振興活動をアクティヴに非営利で継続している。映画祭では、毎回、ASIFA-JAPAN が ASIFA パーティを催し、また、ASIFA ブースも運営して、ASIFA の活動費捻出に協力している。

1997 年 5 月 23 日、役員改選が行なわれ、木下小夜子が会長に選出され、以後再選。
2005 年より、国際アニメーションデー（IAD）の活動にも毎年参加。交換上映用の作品集（DVD）『ASIFA-JAPAN Vol.1』『ASIFA-JAPAN Vol.2』を制作。
2010 年 8 月、HIROSHIMA 2010 にて、映画祭 25 周年と ASIFA50 周年を共に祝い、ASIFA50 周年名誉会長である Raoul Servais 氏をお迎えした。
2010 年 9 月現在、会員 62 名。

ASIFA 日本支部会長
木下　小夜子

YOJI KURI
Interview By Ed Desroches

Yoji Kuri has been an ASIFA member since the beginning of the organization and remains an icon within ASIFA-Japan. His internationally award winning work identified him as one of the leading independent animators in Japan and is wildly different than most animationbeing produced by studios in Japan. His artistic diversity expands beyond animation and into painting, manga, sculpture, writing and picture books.

What was it that put you into the world of animation?
It would take 10 years to discuss the story, but it started for me around the 1950s, about 54 years ago, when I was 28 – I'm now 82 years old. I knew then about the coming of the animation generation. People were all inspired at the time by Walt Disney. And since their work was so famous I wanted to make my own animation.

Sayoko Kinoshita, Yoji Kuri, Renzo Kinoshita, Takae Imajo in Annecy 1993.

Yoji Kuri, Noureddin ZarrinKelk, and Kawamoto during Hiroshima 2000.

Your work is very unique. Where do the ideas for your work come from?

Not from dreams or anyone else's work, they are just my ideas. My ideas usually come from the manga that I used to do for adults.

Whose work do you admire or respect?

I respect a lot of people. When I went to France at the beginning of ASIFA I met Norman McLaren. I respect him and became very good friends with him along with Alexandre Alexeieff, Bruno Bozzetto, Gopo, and George Dunning (who did The Flying Man).

ASIFA Korea General Assembly 2004.

ASIFA KOREA

When I went to the United States in 1971 and started working in the animation industry, I knew that ASIFA was an 'International Animation Film Association', supporting and promoting animation artists throughout the world. However, like other USA companies, I was too occupied with the animation production work to have any special interest in ASIFA.

In 1980, I was working at Marvel Production as a director and line producer for many of TV mini-series, the Transformers series, and the Transformers the Movie. At that time, there were not enough producing companies to cover the increasing demands of productions of USA animation industry, so many of companies looked to outsource their works to countries such as Japan, Korea, Taiwan and so on in order to meet the delivery schedules. The situation at Marvel Production was no different.

In 1985, I came to Seoul to supervise production work. At that time, Korea was doing most of the service work for Japanese animation studios. I brought more work from the U.S.A., which led to the boom of American animation in Korea.

ASIFA KOREA

At this time there was no proper channel of communication and exchange with the animation communities of other countries. As time went on, Korean animation professionals had grown frustrated of doing service works for international studios. They wanted to make their own creations. I decided it was important to do something to improve the future of Korean animation.

It was not an easy road, but in May, 1995, I decided to do two things: publish ANIMATOON magazine for Korean animators, providing them with a window to international animation; the other was to organize ASIFA-Korea to connect with many other countries and improve the quality and creativity of Korean animation.

Once, I tentatively established the name ASIFA-Korea, I flew to Annecy to visit the ASIFA headquarters and meet Michel Ocelot, the ASIFA president at that time. In February 1996, I gathered many animators, professors, independent film directors etc., and told them about ASIFA and its activities. In April, 1996, we had 25 members and were officially approved as a new chapter named ASIFA-Korea.

ASIFA Korea Board Meeting.

2009 IAD - Nelson's opening.

The same year, a newly elected Korean government officially announced their support of the animation industry in order to export Korean cultural contents. As one of their supporting policies, they helped sponsor SICAF (Seoul International Cartoon and Animation Festival) in the hopes of generating more public interest (especially about Korean youths) in animation.

As an international animation institution, ASIFA-Korea participated in and supported many animation events: SICAF, PISAF (Puchon International Student Animation Festival), Anitown Festival in Chunchon, Jeonju Film Festival etc...

The main goal of ASIFA-Korea is to boost animation arts presence in the world and to encourage animation education. Since its beginnings, ASIFA-Korea has held various events: animation artwork exhibitions, academic lectures, animation experience classes, IAD film screening, outside seminars, and open-air screening.

Through these workshops and seminars, prospective animators can learn more practical skills and techniques. Designed specifically for young people, programs are systematically prepared: drawing skills, approach to caricature, understanding action, the principle of animation, consideration of audience level.

Below right: 2007 IAD - reception on the opening day of IAD screening. Below left: 2007 IAD - welcoming visitors for IAD screening.

ASIFA-Korea is composed of various professionals who work in the Korean animation industry: professors, animators, directors and writers. As of 2010, we have a president and founder (Nelson Shin), 2 Vice presidents, 13 general board members, 27 members, a student member and an ASIFA coordinator of the institution. We are always trying to encourage more Korean animation and artists to join ASIFA Korea.

Nelson Shin

Nelson is an animation producer, animator, professor, CEO of AKOM studio, editor-in-chief of ANIMATOON, President of ASIFA Korea and President of ASIFA.

2009 IAD opening - members and VIP visitors.

아시파 코리아의 역사

내가 ASIFA Korea 를 한국에 설립하게 된 역사를 쓰자면 나의 이야기부터 시작하게 된다.

나는 1971 년 미국으로 들어가 애니메이션 일을 했는데, 그 때부터 ASIFA 가 국제애니메이션필름협회로써 창작 애니메이션 예술인들을 위한 세계적인 교류활동을 하고 있다는 것을 어렴풋이 알게 되었다. 그러나 미국 대부분의 회사 일이 그렇듯이 애니메이션제작일로 너무 바빴기 때문에, ASIFA 에 관해서 크게 관심을 두지는 못했다.

나는 San Francisco 에 있는 Animation House 에서 약 1 년간 단편애니메이션 일을 하다가, Hollywood 로 내려와 DePatie-Freleng 회사에서 애니메이터로 있으면서 CF 광고, Star Wars 의 특수효과와 Pink Panther 애니메이션을 했다.

그리고 1980 년 감독으로 Marvel Production 에서 작품개발, CF 광고 그리고 Line Producer 로 TV Mini-Series, the Transformers Series, the Transformers the Movie 등을 제작했다. 이 시기에 미국은 급증한 애니메이션 제작을 감당하기는 역 부족이었다. 미국의 여러 회사들은 이렇게 증가하는 애니메이션을 납기 안에 제작해 내기 위하여, 해외로 필름 제작을 의뢰해야 했다. 그래서 일본, 한국, 대만 등지에 대량으로 보내졌다. 이러한 어려운 상황은 내가 일하고 있는 우리 미국회사도 마찬가지였다.

내가 Marvel 회사의 애니메이션제작 일을 돕기 위해 서울에 다시 나온 것은 1985 년이었는데, 한국에는 일본에서 넘어 온 부분제작은 활발하였고 나는 미국에서 최초로 한국에 OEM 제작을 가져왔고, 미국 애니메이션 작업은 한국에서 선풍적으로 인기를 모았다. 그러나 여전히 한국에서는 애니메이션 창작을 위한 국제적인 교류가 전혀 없었다. 한참 동안 한국에서 Copy Rights 이 없는 해외주문제작을 서비스하면서, 자체적인 비판에 이르게 되었다. 이때 내가 마음먹은 것 2 가지가 있었는데 그 하나는 'ANIMATOON'이라는 애니메이션 정보지를 출간하여 한국의 애니메이션 학도들에게 세계의 애니메이션에 눈 뜨게 해 주는 것이고, 또 하나는 ASIFA 에 합류하여 여러 국가들과 연계하고 애니메이션 창작력을 한국에 심어주는 목표를 세우는 것이었다.

의도를 실행하는 것이 쉽지 않지만, 나는 그 두 가지 일을 결국 해내었다. 1995 년 5 월 가칭 ASIFA Korea 의 결성을 하고, 처음으로 서울에서 프랑스 앙시를 방문하여 ASIFA 본부 위원들을 비롯한 그 당시의 Mitchel Ocelot 위원장을 처음으로 접견했다. 그 이듬해 2 월, 한국의 감독들을 주축으로 애니메이터, 교수, 독립 필름작가, 배경화가 등 예술인들로 구성된 여러 사람들을 불러놓고, 국제 ASIFA 에 관해 소개하고 국제적인 활동의 필요성을 설명했다.

뜻을 같이한 25 명의 창립회원들은 가칭 ASIFA Korea 의 창립 준비를 갖고, ASIFA 국제기구에 새로운 국제회원으로 등록하기로 선언했다. 1996 년 4 월 ASIFA Korea 로 신청했던 국가명칭대로 ASIFA 의 공식승인을 받아냈다.

같은 해, 한국의 새로운 정부에서는, 문화수출산업으로 육성하기위해 애니메이션을 국책사업으로 정하고 SICAF (Seoul International Cartoon and Animation Festival)을 개최하여 만화와 애니메이션에 대한 새로운 인식을 갖게 해 주었으며, 청소년들의 이상과 상상력을 심어 주려는 기회를 늘리고 있었다. 이에 따라 ASIFA Korea 는 SICAF, PISAF (Puchon International Student Animation Festival), Anitown Festival in ChunChon, Jeonju Film Festival 등 수 십여 한국내의 애니메이션 행사를 후원, 협회로서 많은 활동을 펼쳐왔다.

협회는 애니메이션 교육의 일환으로 다양한 워크샵 활동들을 하고 있다. 체험교실실시, 평면그림전시, 강연회, IAD 스크리닝, 야외 세미나와 상영회 등의 행사를 이끌고 있으며, 이러한 워크샵이나 세미나에서는 애니메이션을 좋아하거나 배우고 싶은 청소년들을 위해, 학문보다는 기능과 기술에 대해 설명하고 가르치고 있다.

특히 청소년들을 위해서는 좀 더 조직적으로 가르치기 위해 다음과 같은 카테고리별로 강의를 진행한 다 −데생 기술, 캐리캐처 시각, 액션의 이해, 애니메이션 원리, 그리고 관객의 수준.

또한 조기 교육으로는 어린이들의 상상하는 습관을 심어주기 위해, 상상하는 테마를 그림으로 그리도록 하고 음악을 듣고 자연 과학에 관심을 갖도록 유도하고 있다.

ASIFA Korea 의 조직은 여러 애니메이션 관련 종사들로 구성되어 있다. 교수, 애니메이터, 감독, 작가 등이 속해 있으며, Founder 로 Nelson SHIN 회장, 부회장 2명, 이사 14명, 일반 국제회원 28명, 학생 8명, 간사 1명이 아시파 코리아를 이끌면서 더 많은 회원 유치를 위해 노력하고 있다.

아시파 코리아
회장 넬슨 신

ASIFA POLAND

Wiola Sowa in Hiroshima Festival.

The first Polish filmmaker, who joined the board of ASIFA was Ryszard Brudzyński, for many years the head of the Łódź Film Studio and Studio of Small Film Forms "Se-Ma-For", which he initiated together with Jerzy Mierzejewski. During the congress in 1962 he was elected member of the ASIFA board. Some sources mention that Brudzyński represented Polish film industry already at the 1960 meeting in Annecy. What supports this view is the fact that the vision around which "Se-Ma-For" was organized was close to the idea of National Film Board of Canada, where Norman McLaren created his films.

Ryszard Brudzyński was a writer, satirist, author of scripts for many animated films, among others A Small Quartet by Edward Sturlis and Circus by Włodzimierz Haupe. He was also a visionary and - as remembered by Daniel Szczechura – a manager, who despite financial limitations, took care of the artistic quality of the productions. The experimental and creative atmosphere Brudzyński created lasted long after he was forced to leave his position in 1968. It should be enough to say, that "Se-Ma-For" is the only Polish Film Studio to have received two Academy Awards.

Norman McLaren visited Polish studios in 1959, even before he was chosen president of ASIFA. Up to that moment, Polish animation managed to strengthen as an industry. Separate animated film studios emerged in Łódź, Bielsko- Biała and Warsaw - each with a specific character - and at the Cracow Academy of fine Arts Faculty of Graphic, an animation studio was created.

In the Łódź studio McLaren met filmmakers, students and critics and expressed the hope to continue and develop these contacts. Apart from the idea of communication beyond the steel curtain and political boundaries, he had reasons to take a closer look at Polish animation, which at the time was becoming more and more noticeable in the international arena.

The films of Jan Lenica and Walerian Borowczyk, after their debut in 1957, had already achieved success at major European festivals – in Venice, Mannheim, Brussels. Change of Guard by Włodzimierz Haupe and Halina Bielińska was awarded in Cannes. Also around this time artists such as Mirosław Kijowicz, Daniel Szczechura and Witold Giersz emerged and, shortly after, triumphed at many international film festivals.

Around the time that Lenica and Borowczyk came out, another artist – Jerzy Kotowski -made his debut with the film Caution. He was the second Polish filmmaker after Brudzyński to be chosen member of the ASIFA board in 1973. Kotowski, who graduated at the FAMU faculty of cinematography, had the spirit for experimenting and explored all kinds of techniques and genres. As an artist, he cooperated with the "Se-Ma-For" Studio and as a teacher – with Łódź Film School.

In 1977, on the occasion of 30 years of Polish animated film, Polish filmmakers organized a session in Bielsko Biała, which was joined by the board of ASIFA. The session resulted in the decision to start publishing a magazine of the Society in Poland. The first editor of the quarterly entitled "Animafilm", was Mieczysław Walasek, a film critic, editor and co-founder of the weekly "Ekran" as well as monthlies – "Kamera" and "Studio".

Walasek passed away before the first issue of "Animafilm" appeared. His editorial duties were continued by Marcin Giżycki - at the time young film critic and historian and well as lover of animated film.

The quarterly was in four languages – Polish, English, French and Russian and had an impressive layout. It was issued in Poland until 1981, when Martial Law was declared. Editing of the quarterly was continued by the Italian branch of ASIFA.

In 1978, the late Jerzy Kotowski was replaced in board by Daniel Szczechura, one of most recognized Polish animation artists. He was the second member of the board connected to 'Se-Ma-For', he was also lecturer at the Warsaw Fine Arts Academy, as well as at The Royal Academy of Fine Arts in Ghent and Emily Carr College in Vancouver. At first he replaced the late Jerzy Kotowski in the board. In his next term (probably from 1982 until 1984), he was elected a vice president of the Society. Apart from numerous awards at film festivals, he received the ASIFA Lifetime Achievement Award in Genova and the ASIFA Award for 'the great contribution into the art and development of animated film' in 1990, at the Animated Film Festival in Zagreb. This year, in 2010, we are celebrating another anniversary – that of Daniel Szczechura's artistic work and his 80th birthday.

Jerzy Kucia, one of the most recognized Polish animated film authors, was a member of the board in the years 1985 – 2000, and for two terms, starting in 1994, he was a vice-president of ASIFA. He has received numerous awards at prestigious festivals. His films were presented in New York's MOMA and London's Tate Modern Gallery. At the same time, he was head of the Cracow Academy of Fine Arts Animated Film Studio and initiated and developed the International Animated Film Workshop in Cracow.

In November 2007, during the IFF 'Etiuda&Anima', Jerzy Kucia with the help of Bogusław Zmudziński, director of the festival, initiated a meeting with Thomas Renoldner - member of the board of ASIFA International. The meeting resulted in the creation of a Polish branch of ASIFA along with a temporary board, chaired by Jerzy Kucia.

In 2008, the 'Etiuda&Anima' Festival invited Sayoko Kinoshita - at that time president of ASIFA, to visit the festival and take part in a plenary session of ASIFA-Poland. A new board was chosen: Wiola Sowa – president, Anna Kuklicz, Mariusz Frukacz, Aleksandra Korejwo and Grzegorz Koncewicz. The board was chosen for one year. In 2010 it was chosen again, with Wiola Sowa (president), Agnieszka Kozłowska, Alicja Jodko and Mariusz Frukacz as 4 5 its members. The present board is preparing the celebration of this year's International Animation Day and of the ASIFA anniversary. It also organises screenings, helps in establishing international contacts, consolidates young artists and people who are active in the field of animation, as well as serves as a source of information.

Alicja Jodko (translated by Marta Pajek)

I would like to thank Jerzy Kucia, Daniel Szczechura, Witold Giersz and Marcin Giżycki for help with gathering information for this article.
Alicja Jodko is founder, teacher and supervisor at the stop motion workshop for the youngest - 'Children's Film Studio', which runs since 1986 in the Gallery 'Entropia' in Wrocław.

Clockwise from left: unidentified, Władysław Kraso, unidentified, Romuald Kropat, Ignacy Goncerz, Stefan Kostrzewski, Kostrzewski, Ewa Borowik, Jan Kobuszewski, and Jerzy Kotowski (in an armchair)

Pierwszym filmowcem z Polski, który znalazł się w zarządzie ASIFA, był Ryszard Brudzyński, dyrektor łódzkiej Wytwórni Filmów Fabularnych oraz Studia Małych Form Filmowych "Semafor", którego był inicjatorem i, wraz z Jerzym Mierzejewskim, współzałożycielem. Na kongresie w 1962 został wybrany na członka Administracyjnej Rady Nadzorczej ASIFA. Niewykluczone, że Brudzyński reprezentował polską kinematografię na spotkaniu w Annecy już w roku 1960. Przemawiałby za tym fakt, że wizja, jaka przyświecała mu przy organizacji "Semafora", zbliżona była do kanadyjskiego National Film Board, a więc studia, w którym tworzył Norman McLaren. Ryszard Brudzyński był także literatem, satyrykiem i autorem scenariuszy wielu filmów ani-mowanych, m.in. "Kwarteciku" Edwarda Sturlisa i "Cyrku" Włodzimierza Haupego. Przede wszystkim jednak był wizjonerem i - jak to wspomina prof. Daniel Szczechura - dyrektorem, który nie bacząc na ograniczenia finansowe dbał przede wszystkim o jakość artystyczną produkcji. Sprzyjająca twórczej pracy i eksperymentom atmosfera, jaką wytworzył w wytwórni, pozostała nawet po jego odejściu ze stanowiska, do czego został zmuszony w 1968 roku.

Dość powiedzieć, że "Semafor" jest polskim studiem, w którym powstały dwa filmy uhonorowane Nagrodą Amerykańskiej Akademii Filmowej.

Norman McLaren jeszcze jako przyszły prezydent ASIFA odwiedził polskie studia w 1959 roku. Do tego momentu polska animacja zdążyła już okrzepnąć pod względem produkcyjnym. W Łodzi, Bielsku Białej i Warszawie funkcjonowały samodzielne studia animacji mające własną specyfikę, a w Krakowie przy wydziale grafiki ASP - zaczęła działać Pracownia Filmu Rysunkowego. McLaren spotkał sie w łódzkim studiu z realizatorami, studentami i krytykami, wyrażając przy tym nadzieję na kontynuowanie i rozszerzanie kontaktów. Prócz samej idei międzynarodowej komunikacji ponad żelazną kurtyną i politycznymi granicami miał istotne powody, by przyjżeć się z bliska polskiej animacji, która w tym czasie zaczęła coraz wyraźniej zaznaczać swoją obecność na arenie międzynarodowej.

Filmy Jana Lenicy i Waleriana Borowczyka, po ich wspólnym debiucie w roku 1957, zdążyły już odnieść sukcesy na kluczowych europejskich festiwalach - w Wenecji, Mannheim, Brukseli, a "Zmiana warty" Włodzimierza Haupego i Hanny 6 7 Bielińskiej na festiwalu w Cannes. W tym mniej więcej czasie rozpoczynają swoją karierę artystyczną twórcy tej rangi co Mirosław Kijowicz, Daniel Szczechura, Witold Giersz, by wkrótce święcić triumfy na festiwalach filmowych w Oberhausen, Cannes, Edynburgu, Melbourne, Locarno, Montevideo, Buenos Aires czy Barcelonie.

Równocześnie z Lenicą i Borowczykiem filmem "Ostrożność" zadebiutował Jerzy Kotowski, następny po Brudzyńskim twórca z Polski wybrany na członka Rady Administracyjnej ASIFA w 1973 roku. Kotowski, absolwent wydziału operatorskiego FAMU był twórcą o temperamencie eksperymentatora tworzącym we wszelkich technikach i gatunkach. Związany ze studiem "Semafor" i Łódzką Szkołą Filmową.

W roku 1977 z okazji 30. lecia polskiego filmu animowanego z inicjatywy władz polskiej kinematrografii została zorganizowana w Bielsku Białej uroczysta sesja z udziałem władz ASIFA. Podczas tej sesji zdecydowano o wydawaniu w Polsce pisma Stowarzyszenia. Pierwszym redaktorem kwartalnika "Animafilm" został Mieczysław Walasek, krytyk filmowy, redaktor i współzałożyciel tygodnika "Ekran" oraz miesięczników "Kamera" i "Studio". Niestety Walasek zmarł jeszcze przed ukazaniem się pierwszego numeru kwartalnika. Po nim ster redakcyjny przejął Marcin Giżycki, młody wówczas krytyk i historyk filmu oraz miłośnik animacji, a późniejszy autor książek poświęconych sztuce, w tym nade wszystko sztuce animacji.

Kwartalnik wychodził w czterech językach, prócz polskiego w języku angielskim, francuskim i rosyjskim, posiadał także bardzo bogatą, częściowo kolorową szatę graficzną. W Polsce ukazywał się do momentu wprowadzenia stanu wojennego w 1981 roku. Następnie redagowaniem kwartalnika zajął się włoski oddział ASIFA.

W 1978 roku zmarłego Jerzego Kotowskiego zastąpił jako członek Rady Adnimistracyjnej prof. Daniel Szczechura, jeden z najgłośniejszych artystów polskiej animacji i zarazem kolejny w ASIFA twórca związany z "Semaforem", wykładowca warszawskiej ASP i uczelni zagranicznych, m.in. Królewskiej Akademii Sztuki w Gandawie i Emily Carr College w Vancouver. W następnej kadencji, prawdopodobnie przypadającej w latach 1982-1984, został wybrany wiceprezydentem Stowarzyszenia. Prócz wielu nagród festiwalowych na całym świecie, otrzymał także Nagrodę ASIFA za całokształt twórczości w 1984 w Genui oraz Nagrodę ASIFA "za nieoceniony wkład w sztukę i rozwój filmu animowanego" w 1990 na MFF Animowanych w Zagrzebiu. W bieżącym 2010 roku przypada wspaniały, tak samo okrągły jak ASIFY, jubileusz pracy twóczej profesora Szczechury oraz jego 80. urodziny.

Jerzy Kucia

Danie Szczechura

W latach 1985 - 2000 członkiem zarządu, a przez dwie kolejne kadencje poczynając od roku 1994 wiceprezydentem ASIFA był prof. Jerzy Kucia, jednen z najbardziej znanych na świecie twórców polskiej animacji, laureat niezliczonych nagród na presiżowych festiwalach, kilkukrotny laureat m.in. British Animation Award za najlepszy film animowany roku. Twórca prezentowany w retrospektywach na całym świecie, m.in. w MOMA w Nowym Jorku i Tate Gallery Modern w Londynie, a jednocześnie pedagog kierujący Pracownią Filmu Animowanego w krakowskiej ASP, inicjator i prowadzący międzynarodowe warsztaty animacji w Krakowie.

W listopadzie 2007 podczas MFF "Etiuda & Anima" z inicjatywy prof. Jerzego Kuci i z pomocą Bogusława Zmudzińskiego, dyrektora fetiwalu, odbyło się w Krakowie spotkanie z Thomasem Renoldnerem, członkiem zarządu ASIFA International, na którym podjęto decyzję o utworzeniu polskiego oddziału ASIFA Poland i powołano tymczasowy zarząd pod przewodnictwem prof. Jerzego Kuci. W 2008 roku kiedy to Sayoko Kinoshita, ówczesna prezydentka ASIFA była gościem MFF Etiuda&Anima, odbyło się walne zebranie członków ASIFA Poland i wybrany został nowy zarząd w składzie:

Wiola Sowa – przewodnicząca, Anna Kuklicz, Mariusz Frukacz, Aleksandra Korejwo i Grzegorz Koncewicz. Zarzad został wybrany na ores jednego roku.

W roku 2010 wybrano nowy zarząd ASIFA Poland z Wiolą Sową jako przewodniczącą oraz Agnieszką Kozłowską, Alicją Jodko i Mariuszem Frukaczem - członkami zarządu. Obecny zarząd przygotowuje obchody Międzynarodowego Dnia Animacji w połączeniu z jubileuszem ASFA, 8 organizuje bądź współorganizuje pokazy polskich filmów animowanych, służy kontaktom międzynarodowym, a przede wszystkim stara się konsolidować młodych twórców i osoby powiązane z polskim filmem animowanym, pełniąc rolę łącznika i bazy informacji.

autor: Alicja Jodko

Składam serdeczne podziękowania profesorowi Jerzemu Kuci, profesorowi Danielowi Szczechurze, panu Witoldowi Gierszowi i Marcinowi Giżyckiemu za wszelką pomoc przy pracy nad powyższym tekstem.

From left: Wiola Sowa,
Ed Desroches, Nelson Shin,
Noureddin ZarrinKelk,
Deanna Morse, and Juliette Crochu

ASIFA ROMANIA

We are proud to mention the contribution made by the Romanian animation film representatives in creating and supporting, as members since the beginning, this "huge family bringing together animation film authors, artists, technicians and innovators from around the world", as former ASIFA President Raoul Servais said in 1990.

We rise to pay homage to the founding members, true fathers of the world of animation, who have created and elevated the artistic level of this film genre to the highest standards.

Well-known Romanian filmmaker Ion Popescu Gopo (who won the "Palme d'Or" Award for his film Short History, was a member of the first ASIFA Board, made up of the most important professionals in the world; Gopo also served a vice-president of our association from 1962-1972.

The General Secretariat was established in Paris in 1960 and moved later to Bucharest. During this time General Secretary was Marin Paraianu - director of ANIMAFILM STUDIO and of The Mamaia International Film Festival (1968 and 1970).

First edited in Paris, the Bulletin was next published in Bucharest under the editorial eye of Marin Paraianu and Elvira Anitei, and the financial support offered by the Romanian authorities at the time. The Bulletin headquarters was at ANIMAFILM Studio between 1968 and 1974.

I recall with great joy when my colleagues and I were accepted as members of ASIFA after the Mamaia Festival in 1968. Reviving the idea I expressed in the 1985 ASIFA anniversary magazine issued at the Annecy Festival 25 edition, I may say: « J'ai eu la grande joie d'etre recue par ta genereuse main tendue vers toutes les mains du monde qui dessinent des lignes vivantes ! »

It's time to thank the ASIFA Secretariat – Mrs. Nicole Salomon and Vesna Dovnikovic, to all ASIFA Board members for the support they have offered us over the years. We also express our gratitude to all who worked and achieved many artistic successes, notably the ASIFA Magazine and IAD.

Olimp Varasteanu, Genevieve Georgescu, Marin Paraian.

We need to thank several festival organizers, who have welcomed with warmth and hospitality their guests in, among others, Annecy, Varna, Zagreb, Espinho and especially Hiroshima.

Romanian animation has eventually come out from the shade it has been standing in since 1989. The very proof is this is the International Film Festival held in Bucharest since 2006 « ANIM'EST ».

Let's celebrate the marvelous 50th anniversary of ASIFA sharing a glass of champagne: « Happy Birthday, long and flourishing lives, a great harmony amongst its members. VIVE l'ASIFA !»

Genevieve Georgescu

Genevieve is an animator and ASIFA Board Member.

June1, 1972: Cinema Scala, Laurentiu Sirbu, Victor Antonescu, Genevieve Georgesco, George Sibianu, Olimp Varasteanu, Luminita Cazacu, Tatiana Apahidean.

Top: Energica.
Above: Gopo Drawing 1989.

Noi, grupul ASIFA – România, suntem mândri de aportul pe care l-am adus încă de la începuturile asociaţiei la această „ adevarată familie care reuneşte creatori, artişti, tehnicieni şi iniţiatori ai filmului de animaţie din întreaga lume ", aşa cum a spus Raoul Servais, preşedintele ASIFA în 1990.

Făcând o scurtă istorie a contribuţiei României trebuie să-l menţionăm pe Ion Popescu Gopo, care a fost membru în diferite jurii ale festivalurilor internaţionale, în Comitetul de onoare cu ocazia sărbătoririi a 25 de ani de la înfiinţarea Festivalului de la Annecy, dar cel mai important – a fost vicepreşedinte al ASIFA în perioada 1962-1972. Secretariatul ASIFA, care şi-a avut sediul iniţial la Paris, in 1960, a fost mutat apoi la Bucureşti. Secretar general a fost Marin Pârâianu – director al Studioului ANIMAFILM şi al Festivalului Internaţional al Filmului de la Mamaia (1968 şi 1970). Unii dintre noi, vechi membri ASIFA, încă ne reamintim de acest festival de marcă, care se organiza alternativ cu cel din Annecy.

Apoi, Buletinul ASIFA, editat iniţial la Paris, a trecut sub conducerea lui Marin Pârâianu şi a Elvirei Aniţa. Aceasta datorită sprijinului financiar oferit de autorităţile romāne de la acea vreme. Intre anii 1968 şi 1974 redacţia Buletinului ASIFA s-a aflat la Studioul ANIMAFILM. Printre primii membri romāni ASIFA s-au numărat Ion Popescu Gopo, Bob Călinescu, Olimp Vărăşteanu, Iulian Hermeneanu, George Sibianu, Florin Anghelescu, Adrian Petringenaru. Regizorii romāni au primit de-a lungul timpului o serie de premii dintre care menţionăm: Olimp Vărăşteanu „Leul de argint" la Festivalul filmului de la Veneţia, in 1970, pentru filmul "Variaţiuni" ; Sabin Bălăşa cu filmul "Picătura" a fost premiat cu „Pelicanul de argint" la Festivalul Internaţional al Filmului de la Mamaia in 1970; Laurenţiu Sârbu pentru filmul său "Puiul" a primit „Premiul CIDALC" la Festivalul filmului de la Cracovia in anul 1973 şi Premiul „Lanterna de aur" la Festivalul Filmului de la Teheran.

Putem spune că animaţia românescă a ieşit în sfârşit din conul de umbră în care a fost după 1989. Dovadă a acestei afirmaţii stă şi Festivalul Internaţional de film ANIM'EST, organizat la Bucureşti din anul 2006. Suntem mândri că aparţinem, în continuare, marii familii ASIFA

Genevieve Georgescu

Genevieve is an animator and ASIFA Board Member.

Luminita Cazacu, Genevieve Georgescu, Annie Maillet (Raymond Maillet's wife), Laurentiu Sirbu.

Goposteam Roland Pupaza, Pierette Atanasiu, Eugenia Boroghina, Ion Popescu Gopo, Cecilia Radulescu, Constantin Crihmarel.

Ecce Homo.

A drawing from Rastko Ciric, from left: Bordo, Nikola Majdak, Vesna Dovnikovic, Thomas Renoldner, in front: Darko Markovic, Macedonia, Zoran Simjanovic, Serbia.

BALKANIMA poster for 2011.

ASIFA SERBIA

We are over thirty and travel throughout wonderland of dreams and vistas. Since 1949, when modern Serbian animation was born (Jocić), Belgarde school of animation rises from the authentic tradition of Serbian Surrealistic circle (magazine «The Impossible» in the 30ies of the last century) and Serbian folk heritage, distinguished by fantastic, mythical beings (Majdak, Šajtinac, Petričić, Vlajić, Bikić studio, Ćirić and others). Both inspirations are genuine and have been internationaly appraised at numerous animation and short film festivals. There are also animation film centers in the cities of Novi Sad, Niš, Vranje and Čačak with schools and young filmmakers. We also host «Balkanima» European Animation Film Festival in Belgrade (each September) and IDRAF- International Children Workshop for Animated Film in Vranje (each August).

Božidar Zečević: A Short History of Serbian Animation

Svetkovina vizuelne antropologije

Светковина визуелне антропологије

Могло би се рећи да читава српска модерна анимација потиче из београдске надреалистичке баштине, поетике немогућег, неочекиваног и субверзивног, као одјек укидања граница између стварног и нестварног те вратоломних путовања геогарфијом сна. Друга њена димензија срасла

ASIFA Serbia Board: Borislav Šajtinac, Nikola Majdak, Bozidar Zecevic, Rastko Ciric.

народна веровања. Древни пандемонијум настањује од памтивека српски митски фолкор и креће се зачуђујуће лако овом географијом. У новијим делима београдске школе анимације (Растко Ћирић) јавља се још један моменат: борхесовски лавиринт без средишта, филм сам, кроз чисте и нечисте силе једне изворне инспирације; светковина визуелне антропологије.

Божидар Зечевић: Кратка историја српске анимације

Fantasmagorie Poster 2008.

211

ASIFA
SWITZERLAND

The GSFA (Groupement suisse du film d'animation aka STFG Schweizer Trickfilmgruppe aka ASIFA-Switzerland) was founded in Geneva in 1968. At that time, it was a priority to get recognition for animation as a method of film making by the official institutions which subsidized film productions, and by the festivals such as the National Film Days of Solothurn. At Solothurn, the GSFA members insisted on presenting their animated shorts. Today, the Saturday afternoon animation competition programme is one of the highly appreciated sure values of the festival.

The films in the screenings were kept by the GSFA in order to create an important collection of 16mm short Swiss animated films. The distribution of prints from the collection and the programmes organized by GSFA members helped expose the Swiss public to independent animation.

In order to aid animators who lacked the necessary support for sending films to international festivals, GSFA founded the Festival service in 1992.

Communication
At the beginning, the GSFA newsletter was created using a spirit transfer-printer and clipped single-handed.
In 1975, GSFA joined the entire Swiss film branch in

co-founding Ciné-Bulletin, a joint newsletter published regularly by the Swiss Film Centre.

A decade later, the need for more internal communication within GSFA led to the resurrection of a quarterly newsletter of its own, named Infonews.

In 1996, it was replaced by a newly conceived paper, Animix. The journal has been published until 2009.

Nowadays, the GSFA communicates with an electronic newsletter, as well as its web-page : http://swiss-animation.ch

Presidents

For 25 years, Nag Ansorge was the first president of the GSFA. Robi Engler took over in 1993 until the beginning of 1997,when Jonas Raeber was elected president. In 1999, Rolf Bächler took on the task, followed by Terry Inglese in 2000 and Olivier Riechsteiner in 2002. Zoltan Horvath is the current president (since 2004).

Activities

The main aim of the GSFA is to establish and maintain a network of all people who are active in the field of animation in Switzerland.

Throughout the year, a variety of activities and events allow its members to meet and present their work:

1. Solothurn : Saturday morning GSFA Brunch followed by the Competition programme in the afternoon.

2. General Assembly.

3. Festivals in Solothurn, Annecy, Locarno, Fantoche, Cinématou : special events and accommodation offered to the members.

4. Festivities such as receptions and cocktail parties at appropriate occasions.

5. Special screenings all over the country (films premières, animation short programmes).

6. Activities of Graines d'Animation.

Text by ASIFA-Switzerland.

ASIFA UNITED KINGDOM

We are very proud that ASIFA UK was one of the first groups to be formed when the association started in 1960, John Halas of Halas and Batchelor, one of the founding fathers, ran the chapter single-handed for many years, screening animation films from behind the Iron Curtain that had never been seen in the "free" world.

When Pat Raine Webb joined his company in 1977, she quickly became involved in his ASIFA work. When he retired in 1986 as President of both ASIFA international and ASIFA UK, Pat formed a UK Board of five people, which included Richard Taylor as President and Margot Grimwood as Treasurer.

Many animation companies were established in London at that time and chapter membership reached almost 200. We had some sponsorship and were able to have many functions, film shows, parties, etc, both in London and at festivals. Gradually many companies moved away from London. Most Board members resigned due to other commitments and some members did not renew when we were forced to increase our membership fees.

Pat Raine Webb.

It was left to Pat and me to run things alone. When Pat died suddenly in 2008, I kept things going. Eventually I took on two more directors, Jamie Badminton and Chris White of Karrot Animation, to help out. Their presence enabled us to start thinking again of expansion.

John always issued a one page President's Letter and when Pat took over she started to produce our UK magazine, Dope Sheet, which grew over the years to a regular eight pages. Since the new Board got involved, the last issue was 16 pages and in colour.

We approach the next 50 years with hope and enthusiasm.

Margot Grimwood

Margot is president of ASIFA UK and an ASIFA Board Member.

ASIFA UK Newsletter

Chris White, Margot Grimwood, Jamie Badminton.

ASIFA
ATLANTA(USA)

We can start the story of ASIFA-Atlanta when Linda Simensky moved to Atlanta in 1995 to begin a job at Cartoon Network. Somehow she was also able to run ASIFA-East in NYC, an impressive feat! At the time, the animation industry in Atlanta was not very big. However, in 1996, things slowly began to change when the animation studio, Primal Screen, moved to Atlanta, bringing several animators.

A few women came to Linda to see if they could get a Women in Animation chapter started (among her many achievements, Linda founded the New York chapter). There was a meeting about this at Primal Screen, but observing all the curious guys who were hovering around the meeting room, Linda decided that there should first be an animation group for everyone. Hence, ASIFA-Atlanta was born.

Stephen Mank of Primal Screen provided early leadership and served as the first president of ASIFA-Atlanta (Noeve Warren served as co-president in the very early days, as did Madeline Fan).

In 1999-2000, with Stephen at the helm, ASIFA-Atlanta started with an impressive burst of screenings that included: "ASIFA Declares War" (WWII cartoons), "Canada Drawn" (National Film Board of Canada animation), "Ain't I a Stinker: Cartoons about Cartooning", and "Good Toons Gone Bad".

During this time, ASIFA-Atlanta's annual "Roll Yer Own" was born, an open screening of local student, independent, and professional animation. We continue to have "Roll Yer Own" every year today, although it became so popular that we split the professional animation into its own event, "Blowin' Smoke".

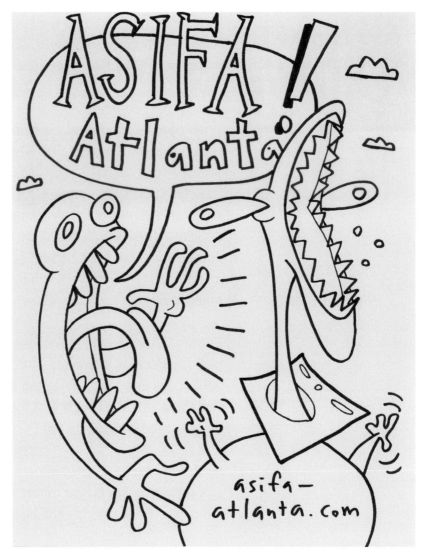

T-shirt design by Brett Thompson

"Roll Yer Own" is our longest running event and has been a staple of the Atlanta animation scene for over a decade. We are grateful to Stephen Mank for starting it!

After Stephen Mank ran ASIFA-Atlanta for about five years, Sarah Fay Krom became president, followed by Lou Hertz, who took over when Sarah moved to Singapore in 2003. Lou helped grow the animation scene in Atlanta by teaching at Atlanta College of Art and Creative Circus and bringing animators into his studio, DESIGNefx. His sense of humour and warm personality touched many Atlanta animators. Lou passed away in 2005 at the age of 73, and ASIFA-Atlanta was briefly dormant.

Joe Peery didn't want to see the organization crumble, so he stepped in, picked up a box of ASIFA stuff from Lou's wife, and became president. Joe already had leadership experience from being involved with the Graphic Artists Guild.

With dedicated board members like Ward Jenkins (screening coordinator), Joe Kubesheski (treasurer), Vella Torres (secretary), Raquel Asturias (membership), and Jennifer Barclay (webmaster), Joe nurtured the animation scene in Atlanta with screenings and the weekly figure drawing class, which began at Primal Screen and is still going strong today. "Roll Yer Own" continued, and we also had a special "Harvey Birdman" screening, among many other events.

Shortly after moving to Atlanta in August 2005, I ran into Joe Peery at a grocery store and asked him about his ASIFA-Atlanta shirt, designed by Ward. "I'd like to get somehow involved with that," I said, and Joe encouragingly replied, "Come on out!"

Karl Sigler and I began to help Joe and Ward with screenings, in particular International Animation Day in 2006, which was held in the basement of Relapse Theater.

Joe Peery.

218

We used Karl's projector, a screen Ward borrowed, and my laptop. With very little promotion, the theatre was almost entirely filled. There was one problem though: the sound didn't work! By chance, a sound engineer friend of Joe's happened to walk in and saved us!

In 2007, ASIFA-Atlanta board member John Ryan talked with the High Museum of Art and we have celebrated International Animation Day there since.

Ward left Atlanta to work for Laika in 2007, and Joe Peery decided to step down from running ASIFA-Atlanta in 2008. I was elected president in February, 2008 and have served since, starting the annual cartoon art show (board member Alena Spragg's idea) and bringing many animation events to Atlanta, such as "Sita Sings the Blues", "Mary & Max", and Don Hertzfeldt. I also co-founded, and continue to curate, the Animation Attack! festival. I also started the monthly Animation Draw event (animation jam sessions open to anyone) and continue to work with the Atlanta Film Festival.

Brett W. Thompson

Brett is an independent animator in Atlanta who served as president of ASIFA-Atlanta from 2008 to 2010.

Brett W, Thompson on stage.

Midwest Animator's Retreat, late 1990's: Jim Middleton, Melissa Bouwman, Deanna Morse, at Starved Rock, IL.

ASIFA CENTRAL(USA)

ASIFA-Central was founded in 1975 as an association of professional and independent animators in Chicago, and has grown to encompass a larger regional area, as the Midwest USA Animation Chapter of ASIFA.

Leadership
Art Pierson was the first President, followed by David Daruszka, who led the chapter for over a dozen years. Deanna Morse served as President for many years, and also was elected to the international board as a representative and a Vice-President. The current President is Jim Middleton. Marla Schweppe and Randy Rockafellow also were Presidents in the mid-90's.

Besides these Presidents, several of the current members have been active in our ASIFA chapter over the decades including Barry Young, Mary Lou Haynes, Jennifer Peterson, Jim Duesing, and Gordon Peterson. Our organization has been fortunate to have these animators working as active volunteers over the years.

Past Activities of note:
In the early 1990's, ASIFA-Central became the first ASIFA

chapter to post a website. Our pioneer webmaster, Byron Grush, received several awards for our site, including an IWAY award, and a citation from Animation Magazine as "one of the top 15 organizations that make a difference."

ASIFA-Central co-sponsored many programs and brought in visiting animators including: Don Bluth, June Foray, Gordon Sheehan, and Shamus Culhane. For years, the chapter coordinated the judging of animation at the Chicago International Film Festival. More recently, ASIFA-Central has worked with the film selection, judging and programming for the Kalamazoo Animation Festival International.

For over a decade, ASIFA-Central held annual weekend retreats at Starved Rock Lodge (Illinois) and in the Chicago area. More recent retreats have been held bi-annually in conjunction with the SMART Festival (Michigan) and the Kalamazoo Animation Festival International (Michigan).

For many years, ASIFA-Central supported the HVH World Peace Storyboard Competition, which gave scholarships to students to create animations envisioning world peace. This program ended a few years ago, but animations created through this initiative have been screened internationally.

Below left: ASIFA/Central Midwest Animator's Retreat, at Wealthy Theatre, Grand Rapids, MI. early 2000's. Front row: Beverly Alger, Angela Mistretta, Jason Roth. Back row: Erik Alexander, Deanna Morse, Jim Middleton. Below right: ASIFA/Central Attendees – early 1990's at Starved Rock.

For decades, the chapter published a regular physical newsletter, Frame-by-Frame. Many of the articles are archived on our website.

Current Activities:
Each year members in at least three different cities have organized screenings and other events in celebration of International Animation Day.

A few members are active in Animation Workshop Group (AWG), and coordinate workshops for children in their home cities (Traverse City, MI: TAP, Chris Allen-Wickler, and Grand Rapids, MI: Deanna Morse and Gretchen Vinnedge). Films created through these workshops have been screened and won awards at international festivals.

ASIFA/Central holds a yearly retreat or event, where members get together for a weekend of festivity, food, fun, and often a bit of square dancing, ghost stories around the campfire, and/or singing. We screen and discuss films, too. Recent retreats have been held in conjunction with the Kalamazoo Animation Festival International, a bi-annual event. On the festival off-years, ASIFA has hosted picnics, field trips and parties, organized when members feel the need for some face-to-face connection and celebration.

ASIFA/Central does not have a home facility, but collaborates with other organizations to present screenings and workshops. Regular collaborators include: TAP (The Art Place) in Traverse City, MI, GRCMC (Grand Rapids Community Media Center) in Grand Rapids, MI, GVSU (Grand Valley State University) in Allendale, MI, KCC (Kellogg Community College) in Battle Creek, MI, Wealthy Theatre in Grand Rapids, MI, and the Kalamazoo International Animation Festival through KVCC in Kalamazoo, MI.

Deanna Morse

Deanna is an independent animator whose diverse work has been screened in festivals, on Sesame Street,

Top: Deanna Morse and Kim White at their Cabin, Starved Rock Lodge, Midwest Animator's retreat, late 1990's

and is represented in permanent collections, including the Metropolitan Museum of Art, New York City, USA. Formerly Vice-President of ASIFA, she is treasurer for ASIFA/Central. She teaches workshops and is a professor at Grand Valley State University, Michigan, USA.

ASIFA/Central Attendees
– 1995 Midwest Animator's
Conference at Starved Rock

Top: Hiking the Trails at Starved Rock, IL, early 1990s. Front: Deanna Morse, Melissa Bouwman. Middle: Jim Schaub, Rich Sharpe. Back: Tony Burda, Jennifer Eldred (Peterson), Fred Bresky.
Middle: Starved Rock, IL where we held our annual retreat for a decade. Angela Mistretta, Jim Middleton, Rose Middleton, Deanna Morse.
Bottom: Some hikers and Attendees of Midwest Animator;s Retreat, Starved Rock Lodge, IL, late 1990's. Kim White, Jennifer Eldred (Peterson), Deanna Morse, Melissa Bouwman, Eric Oehrl, David Baker

ASIFA
COLORADO(USA)

Clip-clop. Clip-clop. The saddle waved from side to side as tumbleweed lazily bumbled across the trail. A small, self-rolled cigarette dangled from the stranger's parched lips. Behind him dust clouds billowed from an army of travellers. Clip-clop. Slowly, horse and rider made their way into town. Eyes peered from behind barrels and barstools and hay bales. Clip-clop. The stranger's eyebrows lifted, smelling it, looking for it, trying to find the goods.

No, this wasn't the gold rush. The year was the beginning of this century and not the beginning of the 1800s. The goods were animators and not gold. The stranger was Edward Bakst and he may not have smoked or rode a horse into Denver, but he found the goods all right. His army was the who's who of international animation. There is a gaggle of animators in Colorado ranging from the very experienced to the simple greenhorns and Edward saw an opportunity to unite them and to promote animation as an art form of personal expression.

Evert Brown discusses a
screening during of films from an
ASIFA-Colorado Workshop.

Edward Bakst settled down in Denver and one by one started calling in his army hoping to recruit more to the ranks. But it was just that, a rush. There needed to be more than just a wayward approach or Edward's efforts would be wasted. The fear being that all the animators in the area would soon depart without having an animation incubator with which to grow and learn and teach. Enter ASIFA. ASIFA gave Edward the vehicle needed to carry all the animators that had been gathering and give them the momentum to move forward. Edward first assembled a core team consisting of folks like Evert Brown, a 30 year animation veteran, Todd Debrecini of Paradigm Ranch, Susan Pivoda of Rocky Mountain College of Art & Design, and Judy Gardner of Gardner Animation Specialists, Ltd.

It took the team about 4 months to lay the groundwork and get the paperwork completed. This included setting up by-laws, incorporating and getting non-profit status with the IRS. They then took out their six-guns and fired life, not death, into the animation underworld that is Colorado. Presenters from all over the world came to talk about who they are, where they are, and where they are going. Initially, membership started with 20 and grew quickly to over 50 animators.

That was then.

ASIFA-Colorado Workshop during the Starz Denver Film Festival 2009.

The idea was great. Bring the who's who out to Colorado and let the animators thrive on the knowledge sharing. But the roadblock was overwhelming. Money. Maybe it could have been solved by the gold rush, but the real question was who would support the influx of presenters. Rocky Mountain College of Art & Design (RMCAD) stepped up to plate and seemed to be willing to foot the bill until the chapter could take care of its own. The problem with that approach was that it immediately alienated the other colleges and animation programs in the area who then saw ASIFA as nothing more than a big sales pitch for RMCAD. This put RMCAD in an awkward position because the struggling ASIFA Chapter was not growing fast enough to support itself.

Mark Hubley helps out during an ASIFA-Colorado Workshop.

Then there was the art itself. While animation as a form of expression is a wonderful concept, the American landscape is not ready for animation solely for the sake of animation. Unfortunately, the promotion of art in the United States of America is a difficult task unless it is based on commercialism. There is rarely any money for pure art and grants are sparse and difficult to attain. This meant that very few companies in the area would be interested in expressionistic animation unless it solved their problem, which is to survive.

This is now.

There is a saving grace. Some folks of the original board have remained, steadfast and stalwart. After Edward Bakst rode off into the sunset (or in this case more like the sunrise) some of the momentum went with him. The original board members have had a difficult time raising money and attracting animators and presenters. But they see ASIFA as an opportunity to unite and keep united the animators looking for a gathering well, a place where thoughts and techniques could be shared, networking performed, and workshops held. "It began for all the right reasons," said Todd Debrecini, one of the founding members.

Today ASIFA-Colorado has a strong membership base and it is continually growing – now almost at 50 members. The chapter is held together by its monthly events, annual parties, and of course, its workshops. The monthly events include presentations by animators, directors and producers as well as screenings and drawing get-togethers. Our annual parties include a summer barbecue and a winter beer tent networking event. And our workshops include an annual competition and workshops at the Starz Denver Film Festival, many children's workshops, web workshops, and adult stop motion workshops as part of the GI Joe Film Festival.

We've teamed up with many other non-profit groups to put our events and workshops together. Our partners include Boulder Digital Arts, Denver Film Society and Alliance of

Joey Buhrer abd Judy Gardner during Animation Station 2009.

Illustrators and Graphic Artists. We are always looking for more opportunities to share our knowledge and art with these other groups.

With the current board behind the reigns, the vision is to keep the ASIFA Chapter in Colorado. The consensus of the current ASIFA-Colorado board is to present all forms of animation, thereby keeping all animators of the community involved, informed and internationally aware of the art that is animation. They would like to cultivate and promote animation as an art, craft and profession. This they expect to do by stimulating discussions about industry, making the Colorado Region a viable option for commercial productions around the world, building a tradition of popular events, creating a link between professionals and students, and bringing international diversity into the arena. In other words, they would like to continue on the path set by Edward Bakst whose efforts were needed and powerful. But they want a larger path, one that includes animation for art, animation for entertainment and also, animation in commercialism.

The trail is dusty and dirty. Life under the stars is not as glamorous as the trail hands once thought. But the members are now wary, street-smart, curious, and experienced to the trail that lay before them. Camp is prepared artfully and diligently before the horses are put to bed. Clip-clop.

Ed Desroches

Ed is a Vice President of ASIFA and President of ASIFA-Colorado. Aside from working in animation, digital editing, and web design and development Ed regularly holds children's animation workshops. He is an expert marksman and pacifist along with having a degree in eternal optimism.

From left: Evert Brown, Ed Desroches, Wes Price, and Joey Buhrer before the ASIFA-Colorado Animation Station Workshops 2009.

EVERT BROWN

Interview By Ed Desroches

Evert Brown is an Emmy Award winning director and a long standing ASIFA member, first with ASIFA-Hollywood. He co-founded ASIFA-Colorado where he has been on the board since its inception.

How did you get started in animation?

It was a fluke. I knew of the company, Bill Melendez Productions, having worked on this corporate design with a designer, Steve Smith. I knew some of the artists who worked at Bill's and one day on the way back from a job interview I stopped in to say hello. They said that Bill was out of town, but did I want to do a few drawings for a commercial they were working on. 'Sure', I said, and then I came back and did more, then Bill came back into town and asked if I wanted to stay on and work on the shows. I stayed for 30 years.

Was working for Bill Melendez your first job?

It was my first in the animation industry. I went to the Chouinard Art Institute and took a lot of drawing classes. That ability really paid off in being able to draw the Peanuts characters.

What type of work did you do there?

Over the 30 year span, I did every job there was. Story and layout were my real strong jobs, but I did backgrounds, animation, character design and painting. I didn't do too much editing, that was a bit to technical. I did editing on my own films, in super 8 film, the real small, stuff.

Did you have a specific character you worked on with Peanuts?

No, I did them all. We weren't a big enough company to split up characters like Disney does.

Did you work on other cartoons besides Peanuts?

Quite a few, we worked on many shows where we designed the characters.
We did a half hour show where I designed the characters and the Yes, Virginia, There is a Santa Claus show won an Emmy. I also directed three Cathy half hours shows, the first won an Emmy. We did the first two Garfield shows which went on to become an empire for Phil Roman.

What type of work are you doing in Colorado?

I have done one commercial that came through my website from some folks that I worked with in Hollywood. They were in Florida, and I hired some students to help out because of the low budget. It worked out great and can be seen on my web site, www.animationman.com.

Evert Brown after announcing the winners of the 2007 Animation Station competition.

Evert Brown at his drawing table in front of his Emmy.

ASIFA-East dinner for Animators Society Honoree Nick Tafuri, (c. 1978-79). Left to right: Howard and Iris Beckerman, Doug Crane, Candy Kugel, Ed Smith.

ASIFA EAST(USA)

As ASIFA celebrates its 50th birthday, ASIFA-East celebrates its 45th. ASIFA-East serves the animation communities along the United States' northern to mid-Atlantic coast, from Maine to Pennsylvania. We are, after ASIFA-Hollywood, the largest ASIFA National Group, with a membership of approximately 300. ASIFA-East also has the proud distinction of hosting, since 1969, the longest-running animation festival in America.

The US animation industry was born in ASIFA-East territory: America's first entertainment shorts by John Stuart Blackton and the Edison studio, Winsor McCay, Emile Cohl and Eclair, J.R. Bray, Earl Hurd, Barré-Bowers, The Hearst studio, Otto Messmer and the Sullivan studio, the Fleischers, and Paul Terry, were all made in New York and New Jersey. After theatrical short production in the 1930s shifted largely to the West Coast, the Terry and Paramount studios continued producing shorts in New York until the last days of theatrical cartoon production in the 1960s.

From the late 40s, New York, as the country's advertising hub, emerged as creative hotbed of television advertising. Top animation talent drifted steadily from Hollywood studios back to the East Coast to work and to set up shop: Shamus Culhane, John and Faith Hubley, Grim Natwick, Bill Tytla, Gene Deitch, Preston Blair, Don Duga, and Jack Zander were a few of these celebrated and enduring artists. Their talent and vision shaped a generation of renowned television commercials and shows.

New York has also long distinguished itself as fertile ground for independent animation. From the 1930s until today, internationally celebrated independent animators, from Norman McLaren and Mary Ellen Bute to Ernest Pintoff, the Hubleys, Jimmy Picker, John Canemaker, John Dilworth, Bill Plympton, and scores of others, have found Gotham irresistible, and something of New York's grittiness has permeated their work.

In a more recent and remarkable development, a startling number of independent feature-length theatrical films substantially, often even entirely, animated by one person have been produced by ASIFA-East artists, including Plympton, Xeth Feinberg, Nina Paley, and Paul and Sandra Fierlinger.

ASIFA-East members at Cedar's Tavern (c. 1990). Left-to right: David Ehrlich, John Dilworth, Howard Beckerman, Janet Benn, Linda Simensky, Tom Warburton, Vince Cafarelli, Candy Kugel, Ronen Divon, unidentified.

ASIFA-East was founded in 1965. Animator Howard Beckerman recalls that the occasion was marked by a special visit from Pierre Barbin, secretary-general of ASIFA and director of the fledgling Annecy Festival. ASIFA-East's founding and Barbin's visit were fêted with a large reception at the Huntington Hartford Museum in Columbus Circle. Among the attendees, Beckerman remembers, were former international ASIFA president John Hubley and eminent film critic Stanley Kaufman. On June 3, 1966, in his initial public announcement of the Group, ASIFA-East's first president Shamus Culhane wrote that the new Group "would provide a center for information on international film festivals, as well as organize such festivals here in New York."

Though of course a central mission of ASIFA is, through the universal art of animation, to transcend international borders and barriers, it seems not everyone always agreed with this ideal: Dick Rauh, ASIFA-East's president from 1968 to 1991, remembers, "There was some dissension in the beginning from some of the local animators because they thought the international was too radical (allowing Russia and Yugoslavia to be represented, for example), but that calmed down after a while."

ASIFA-East held screenings anywhere from the Museum of Modern Art and the Society of Illustrators to hotel meeting rooms. Even upstairs rooms at Schrafft's restaurants, suitably equipped by hauling a 16mm projector up the stairs, became ASIFA screening rooms ("All the Schrafft's that we used went out of business," says Beckerman). Notable attendees of this period, Beckerman remembers, included notorious tabloid photographer-filmmaker Weegee, puppeteer Bil Baird and multimedia artist Red Grooms as well as visiting animators from around the world.

Culhane's proposal to create a festival came true in three short years. In 1969, Rauh, animator Pete Dekas, and others launched the ASIFA-East Animation Festival. We have held this festival every year since. Many Oscar winning or nominated films premiered at our festival, yet we have doggedly resisted the trappings of tuxedos and celebrity juries. Any ASIFA-East member may vote on the films, and many a deserving film that might escape a more mainstream festival has found its audience.

Linda Simensky succeeded Rauh as president in 1991 and was followed, in 2000, by Dave Levy. ASIFA-East International Board members to date have included Beckerman (from circa 1987-1992), David Ehrlich (from 1992-2003) and this writer (from 2003 to present). However, ASIFA-East's most influential members and their contributions have generally far exceeded the scope of their formal roles.

Animator Tissa David, ASIFA-East treasurer for many years, ran and "continued to run the festival for a long time after I took over," says Simensky, "She was detail-oriented and had opinions on everything from the winners on down to the types of cheese we would buy for the reception. But I appreciated that—I felt that ASIFA was as much about tradition as about animation, and I liked that the group had a sense of history." Bill Lorenzo, longtime news-letter editor, frequently wrote, typed, and pasted up entire issues singlehandedly. Countless others have managed the

ASIFA-East Festival (late 1990s). Left to right: Dave Levy, Sheng Huang, Nourii Zander, Jimmy Picker, Vince Cafarelli, Candy Kugel.

newsletter, website, and festival. Rauh, Michael Sporn, John Gati, Candy Kugel, and Beckerman have contributed office space. Others have arranged and curated screenings and events—too many to list—although Lorenzo, Ehrlich, Beckerman, and Rauh have over the years likely made the longest-running and most diverse contributions to our events calendar. Ehrlich also spearheaded the international collaborative films Academy Leader Variations (1987) and Animated Self-Portraits (1989).

Today, our events include screenings, panels, figure-drawing classes, and an animation art auction as well as the special programs and visits that reach us from ASIFA National Groups around the world. "It's wonderful to be swapping programs with other international groups each year, as well as celebrating International Animation Day every October," says Levy. "I really appreciate what International does to foster a world community, something that local chapters can't do in the same way."

"I thought [ASIFA-East]'s strength in many ways was that someone from the animation industry from anywhere in the world could show up in New York and, if they attended an ASIFA event, they'd know people and feel that they were

Motion Picture Academy Oscar-Nominated Animated Shorts screening (c. 2006). Left to right: Vince Cafareli, Candy Kugel, Jimmy Picker, Frank Mouris, Michael Sporn, John Dilworth.

among friends," says Simensky. I also liked being part of a group that had grass-roots impact but was also part of a larger international group."

"Nothing quite replaces taking an active part in a genuine community," says Levy. "That said, we're always searching for ways to stay relevant, to meet and exceed the needs of this community. It's a never-ending job. If it wasn't, we'd be doing something wrong."

ASIFA-East has, for 45 years, been a special group. With continued dedication—and perhaps a little luck to go with it—our group has every hope to keep doing that never-ending job a good 45 more years from now.

Ray Kosarin

Ray produces, directs, and animates for television and film. He has directed or supervising directed on many TV series in the US and Europe including Daria, The World of Tosh, and Beavis and Butt-Head. He is an ASIFA Board Member.

ASIFA HOLLYWOOD(USA)

Over the course of five decades, ASIFA-Hollywood has dedicated itself to being one of the premiere organizations in the world promoting the art and industry of animation. From its inception in the early 1960s, ASIFA-Hollywood has managed to set trends and establish institutions, and even launch an industry or two. Animation cels were not considered collectible art until ASIFA-Hollywood began to offer them for sale to the public. Awards were given to animation only on a token basis until the creation of the Annie Awards. Both of these innovations were the creations of the guiding force of ASIFA-Hollywood, June Foray. But there is so much more to ASIFA-Hollywood's story: historic screenings and presentations; classes; AniFest; the Animation Opportunities Expo; film preservation; the Animation Educator's Forum, a world-class archive; and publications such as The Inbetweener and Grafitti, just to name a few of our more visible activities. The list of people who have been involved with ASIFA-Hollywood in the past is a virtual who's who in animation: June Foray, Bill Scott, Steven Bosustow, Ward Kimball, Frank and Ollie, Chuck Jones, Bill Littlejohn and many more.

The headquarters of ASIFA-Hollywood in Burbank, CA

The goals of the organization guide ASIFA-Hollywood's activities:

- To support and encourage animation education
- To support the preservation and critical evaluation of animation history
- To recognize the achievement of excellence in the art and industry of animation
- To increase public awareness of animation
- To act as a liaison to encourage the free exchange of ideas within the animation community
- To encourage journalism documenting current trends and activities in animation

ASIFA-Hollywood's annual Annie Awards honors outstanding achievements and excellence in the field of animation.

- To encourage the social interaction of professional and non-professional animation enthusiasts
- To encourage the development and expression of all forms of animation

ASIFA-Hollywood moved into its first dedicated home in the organization's three-decade life: the ASIFA-Hollywood Animation Center in Burbank, which opened its doors March 26, 1993. Prior to that ASIFA had occupied a series of temporary offices all over the map of Los Angeles, but with the establishment of more permanent digs the organization was able to offer a wide variety of programs to its members. These included screenings, gallery exhibits, filmmaker forums, and classes. Today, the Animation Center also houses the ASIFA-Hollywood Animation Archive.

There is no question that ASIFA-Hollywood has grown remarkably in its first five decades, but there is equally no question that it will continue to grow and prosper in the coming years. For those dedicated the art and industry of animation, the best is undoubtedly yet to come.

Michael Mallory

Michael Mallory is a longtime friend and former board member of ASIFA-Hollywood. He is a writer with numerous books to his credit, as well as countless articles for ASIFA-Hollywood publications and the trades.

ASIFA-Hollywood's archive director Stephen Worth, the legendary June Foray, and ASIFA-Hollywood President Antran Manoogian

A group of animators meet at the ASIFA-Hollywood Animation Archive to study and exchange ideas.

ASIFA PORTLAND(USA)

Set in the mossy Pacific Northwest, the city of Portland, Oregon enjoys a decades-old animation scene known for ground-breaking independents, big-budget feature film-making, and the world-class Platform animation festival. Award-winning independent animators Joan C. Gratz, Rose Bond, Joanna Priestley, Will Vinton, Chel White, David Daniels, Laura DiTrapani, Marilyn Zornado, and more, call Portland home.

The area also boasts studios ranging from boutique to behemoth, including Bent Image Lab, Hinge Digital, Happy Trails Animation, Fashionbuddha, Free Will Enterprises, and LAIKA, where work is underway on a feature to repeat the success of 2009's Coraline.

Simply put, this is a great place to be an animator. ASIFA Portland was formed by and for this unique community over thirty years ago. With dozens of members, the chapter keeps active with screenings, workshops, lectures, socials, art jams, and more.

Mike A. Smith

Mike is President of ASIFA-Portland and ASIFA Board Member.

Right: ASIFA-Portland's Drinking and Drawing Animation Jam. Below: ASIFA-Portland members pose with Adam Elliot (center).

ASIFA
SAN FRANCISCO
(USA)

Left to right: Hohn Hays president, Phil Robinson co-founder, director; J.J. Sedelmajer visiting from NY, Ken Pontac animation director and script writer (from Happy Tree Friends to Bump in the Night, Karl Cohen pres. of ASIFA - occasion was a visit to SF by JJ at Wildbrain 2007.

ASIFA-San Francisco is a very active chapter made primarily of professionals working in the Bay Area animation industry, along with an active contingent of animation students and people who are interested in seeing animated films that they would not otherwise have the opportunity to watch.

Our President, Karl Cohen, organizes monthly programs ranging from screenings of historic works, contemporary programs such as our two programs devoted to recent work by our chapter members, and the annual best of ASIFA/East screening. Each year the chapter celebrates International Animation Day with Ron Diamond's Show of Shows, which presents the best of contemporary animation.

Ron Seawright, Prescott Wright, Geraldine Clarke (Ferks)

Bill Plympton with Marty McNamara at the party for Bill at Carl's Fine Films.

Tara Behym & Nancy Denney-Phelps wearing gardenias at the party for Alexksey Budovsky. Tara is our chapter's vice president and an independent animator who graduated from CAL Arts. Taken in 2004

Richard Williams surrounded by students after he presented a program for ASIFA-SF in 2008

Suzie Templeton showing DeAnza students at an ASIFA event how she animated something a week before she won her Oscar, 2008.

Suzie Templeton.

The annual Careers in Animation event is designed for students to meet and interact with professionals from major Bay Area Studios such as Pixar and ILM. Whenever there are well known animators visiting the Bay Area, like Richard Williams or Adam Elliot just to name two, we hold screenings of their works along with question and answer sessions. We try to combine this with a social event so that our members will have a chance to meet and talk informally with the guest.

Two of our most important services are our newsletter and website. The monthly newsletter, edited by Karl Cohen, covers animation news from the Bay Area and around the world. The newsletter is sent to each chapter member as part of their yearly membership fee. We also maintain a website, The Cable Cartoon, http://www.asifa-sf.org where late breaking events and news items are listed.

Nancy Phelps

Nancy Phelps is an ASIFA Board Member.

NYC animator, Alexksey Budovsky(front) at a party with ASIFA-SF members in 2004. Nancy Denney-Phelps is (on the right) standing back unidentified woman(lower). Litz Plummer, an opera singer(on the left).

Henry Selick talking to Karl Cohen at a reception for Henry after an ASIFA-SF event, 2009.

KARL COHEN

A Personal Appreciation
written before Karl received
the 2008 ASIFA Laureate Award
by Nancy Phelps.

Karl Cohen.

As a fellow member of ASIFA-San Francisco, and a friend of Karl Cohen's for many years, I am thrilled that he has received the 2008 ASIFA Laureate Award.

Karl, a true Renaissance man of animation, is a historian, notable collector of animated films, and author of many authoritative articles published in periodicals throughout the world. He is a professor of animation history at San Francisco State University and the author of *Forbidden Animation: Censored Cartoons and Black Listed Animators in America*.

Last, but not least, Karl has been the president and guiding light of ASIFA-San Francisco for over two decades. The ASIFA-San Francisco newsletter, for which Karl is editor and primary writer, is read by animation fans around the world for the wealth of information he gathers each month.

Despite his busy schedule, our Laureate is never too busy to ignore a request for information or to share a new film discovery with friends and colleagues. Bill Dennis, president emeritus of ASIFA-India, considers Karl "a friend, colleague, and all-around 'prince of animation'. We all know Karl as a great writer and master of animation history. We know him as a man of principle and a staunch supporter of ASIFA. But, for me, his most enduring attribute is how he values, nurtures, and protects his friendships. What a rare quality!"

In the early 1970's Karl was part of the team of light artists that created mind-blowing visuals for Bill Graham's famous rock concerts at the Fillmore Auditorium. Later in the 70's and 80's, he presented a weekly film and animation program at Intersection for the Arts, San Francisco's oldest alternative art space, where such well-known personalities as Father Guido Sarducci and Robin Williams got their start.

Karl combined his love of animation history and keen interest in politics in his 1997 book, *Forbidden Animation: Censored Cartoons and Black Listed Animators in America*, an invaluable reference and a must for any serious student of animation. He is currently at work on a new book, Animated Propaganda During the Cold War, which will take an in-depth look at the political exploitation of animation on both sides of the Iron Curtain.

Tsvika Oren, lecturer at Bezalel University and president of ASIFA-Israel, remembers his first visit to Karl's home: "Never have I ever seen such a huge private collection of 16mm prints." He goes on to say, "For anyone addicted to animation, it is most recommended to have Karl Cohen as an animation 'pusher'. For many years now I've been one of the many addicts enjoying the prime stuff Karl generously distributes. Since it's such healthy stuff, I've been passing it on for years."

As much as his film knowledge and writings are appreciated around the world, Karl's most substantial and sustained contribution to the San Francisco animation community is his continuing work as president of ASIFA-San Francisco, one of the oldest and most active chapters in the world, with monthly screenings of professional and student's work. The list of international film community members who have gone out of their way to visit Karl covers the entire world, and Karl never fails to have an ASIFA event to welcome them and share their talents with our members. Of course, this always includes one of our chapter's fabulous parties.

Karl's support of independent animators is legendary and best summed up by award-winning New York animator Nina Paley: "There is only one Karl. I wish that we had one in New York! He is animation's best ally. Boundless passion for the art, mixed with intelligence, scholarship, taste, and the discipline to keep putting it in writing year after year . . . .. Like us independent animators, he is driven by his love of the art, not money. He wants us all to succeed, he wants animation to be seen and loved and respected. In everything he writes he has only the progress, survival, and preservation of our art as his goal. I love that man."

In spite of Karl's many activities, he still finds time to be a true friend to all of us who are lucky enough to know him. He and I have spent many hours talking about everything under the sun, but first and foremost sharing our love of animation. The only regret I have about moving to Belgium is that I miss my daily phone chats with Karl. Karl is my mentor and my editor, but first and foremost he will always be my dearest friend. It is very fitting that Karl Cohen join such illustrious names in the world of animation as Karl Zeman, Bob Godfrey, Raoul Servais, and Normand Roger as an ASIFA Laureate.

Richard Williams and Karl Cohen.

ASIFA REPRESENTATIVES AND CONTACT PERSONS

Contact Persons

Asia - Sayoko Kinoshita
Africa and Arab countries – Mohamed Ghazala
South America – Oscar Mario Desplats

ASIFA Magazine – Ray Kosarin
ASIFA NET – Thomas Renoldner
Film Archive - Tsvika Oren
Animation Festivals - Heikki Jokinen
Education - Deanna Morse
International Animation Day – Juliette Crochu
ASIFA Advisor and Liaison for Animators in
Developing Countries – Nancy Denney Phelps
ASIFA Workshop Group – Anastasia Dimitra

Honorary Board

Honorary Secretary General – Nicole Salomon

ASIFA NATIONAL GROUPS

**Representatives of ASIFA National Groups and
MEMBERS OF THE ASIFA BOARD OF DIRECTORS**

AFCA – ASIFA FRANCE ······· Juliette CROCHU
ARGENTINA ················ Oscar M. DESPLATS
AUSTRIA ················· Thomas RENOLDNER
BOSNIA & HERZEGOVINA ····· Berin TUZLIC
BULGARIA ················ Pencho KUNCHEV
CARIBBEAN ··············· Camille SELVON ABRAHAMS
CHINA ··················· Johnchill LEE
COLOMBIA ················ Ricardo ARCE
CROATIA ················· Vesna DOVNIKOVIC / **Secretary General**
EGYPT ··················· Mohamed GHAZALA
FINLAND ················· Heikki JOKINEN / **Vice President**
GREECE ·················· Anastasia DIMITRA / **Treasurer**
HUNGARY ················· Tamas PATROVITS
INDIA ··················· Bill DENNIS
INDONESIA ··············· Gotot PRAKOSA
IRAN ···················· Noureddin ZARRINKELK
ISRAEL ·················· Tsvika OREN
ITALY ··················· Luca Raffaelli
JAPAN ··················· Sayoko KINOSHITA / **Vice President**
KOREA ··················· Nelson SHIN / **PRESIDENT**
MEXICO ·················· Jose Carlos Garcia de LETONA
POLAND ·················· Wioletta SOWA
ROMANIA ················· Genevieve GEORGESCO
SERBIA ·················· Bozidar ZECEVIC
SWITZERLAND ············· Elisabeth SENFF
UNITED KINGDOM ·········· Margot GRIMWOOD
USA ATLANTA ············· Brett W. THOMPSON
USA CENTRAL ············· Deanna MORSE
USA COLORADO ··········· Ed DESROCHES / **Vice President**
USA EAST ················ Ray KOSARIN
USA HOLLYWOOD ··········· Antran MANOOGIAN / **Vice President**
USA NORTHWEST ··········· PORTLAND – Mike SMITH
                          SEATTLE - Natt THANGVIJIT
USA SAN FRANCISCO ········ Nancy DENNEY PHELPS

What ASIFA
Has Meant to Me

In 1960 by small group of strongly independent animation artists from throughout the world created the International Animators Association (ASIFA). The intent was to create an association of individual artists to propagate the ART as opposed to the COMMERCE of animation. The initial vision was that ASIFA could reach into the media, the schools, the cultural ministries, and make the world community aware of all the wonderful animated films being made, thereby encouraging the furtherance of fine animation into the future. ASIFA initiated and nurtured animation festivals throughout the world. It organized exchange visits by artists from west to east and back, and in its most ambitious (and continuously successful) initiative, it developed animation workshops for children around the world and created collaboration projects to bring children from different lands together.

David Ehrlich

I joined ASIFA-East, the New York local branch of ASIFA in 1975. I had met Howard Beckerman earlier that year, and he suggested I join ASIFA-East and to submit my abstract animation to its festival. Not only did I do so, but by 1977 I began sending my films to other ASIFA-sponsored festivals in Annecy, Zagreb and Ottawa.

In 1979, after some initial success with festival selection committees, I swallowed my shyness and flew to Europe for festivals in Krakow and Annecy. These festivals opened

Taking a break at Zagreb 1988.

Jerzy Kucia, Nikolas Majdek, David Ehrlich - Hiroshima 1994.

my life to the rich world outside and to those people from around the world who became my good friends. Nicole Salomon in particular encouraged my workshops with children in Vermont and throughout the world and brought me into ASIFA. In 1982 at Zagreb, Nicole was elected Vice-President of ASIFA whereupon she organized ASIFA Committee No. 5 on Workshops, a Committee that became tremendously important for my work and for my growing connection to ASIFA on an international level.

I began going to more and more festivals abroad, meeting more of the people who became my friends, inviting them to the U.S. to give children's workshops with me, to screen animated films from their countries, and eventually, to join me on creative ASIFA-Presents collaboration projects. ASIFA has changed in the 50 years since those first great artists sketched out its identity, but what has remained constant through all these years has been its implicit encouragement of international friendships, and it is for this I am most grateful.

David Ehrlich

David Ehrlich is an ex-ASIFA vice president and an ASIFA Prize winner.

IAD POSTERS
INTERNATIONAL
ANIMATION
DAY

2002

Daniela Bak

2003

Iouri Tcherenkov

2004

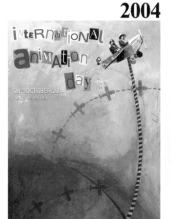

Eric Ledune

2005

Paul Driessen

2006

Noureddin Zarrinkelk

2007

Abi Feijo

2008

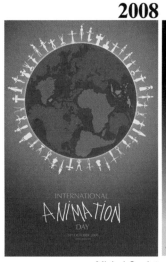

Michel Ocelot

2009

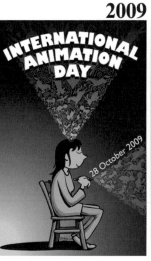

Nina Paley

2010

Raoul Servais

2011

Ihab Shaker

ASIFA **50**th ANNIVERSARY

International Animated Film Association

ASIFA stands for Association Internationale du Film d'Animation.
founded in 1960 in Annecy (France) by the most famous animation artists of that time.
Today the association has more than 60 countries all over the world.

ASIFA CARTOONS

Luminita Cazacu

Bordo Dovnikovic

Ion Truica

Genevieve Georgesco

Mihai Surubaru

CONTRIBUTORS

ASIFA would like to sincerely thank the following companies
and individuals for their assistance in the creation of this book.

Sponsors

The Global Leader in Digital Content and Animation Software
beta.toonboom.com

AKOM PRODUCTION CO.

Nelson Shin

Sayoko Kinoshita

Anastasia Dimitra

Ed Desroches

Mohamed Ghazala

CONTRIBUTORS CONTINUED

Editors

Editor in Chief: Ed Desroches
Editors: Nelson Shin, Chris Robinson
Cover design: Nelson Shin
Page design: Nelson Shin, Ed Desroches

Assistant Editors

Deanna Morse
Jamie Badminton
Juliette Crochu
Margot Grimwood
Nancy Denney-Phelps
Noureddin ZarrinKelk
Thomas Renoldner
Tsvika Oren
Vesna Dovnikovic

Articles

Alfio Bastiancich
Anastasia Dimitra
Anni Lang
Antonio Gaio
Berin Tuzlic
Bill Dennis
Bozidar Zecevic
Brett W. Thompson
Chris Robinson
Christel Degros
Clare Kitson
David Ehrlich
Deanna Morse
Ed Desroches
Elisabeth Senff

Genevieve Georgescu
Heikki Jokinen
Johnchill Lee
Juliette Crochu
Karl Cohen
Luca Raffaelli
Margit Buba Antauer
Margot Grimwood
Michael Mallory
Mike Smith
Mohamed Ghazala
Nancy Denney-Phelps
Nelson Shin
Nicole Salomon
Noureddin ZarrinKelk
Olivier Catherin
Olivier Cotte
Oscar Desplats
Pencho Kunchev
Raoul Servais
Ray Kosarin
Sayoko Kinoshita
Steven Subotnick
Thomas Renoldner
Tsvika Oren
Vesna Dovnikovic
Vivien Halas
Wiola Sowa

Pictures

A & Y Yoresh
Ahmed Ghadyani
Alfio Bastiancich
Amit Aidasani
Anastasia Dimitra
Avi Ofer
Berin Tuzlic
Borivoj Dovnikovic
Bozidar Zecevic
Brett W. Thompson
Candy Kugel
Charles Zee
Chris Robinson
Christel Degros
Clare Kitson
Cristina Lima
David Brunskill
David Ehrlich
Deanna Morse
Ed Desroches
Edo Lukman
Evert Brown
Genevieve Georgesco
Heikki Jokinen
Ion Truica
Isabelle Cracco
Johnchill Lee
Juliette Crochu
Karl Cohen
Leila Ranjbar
Luca Raffaelli

Luminita Cazacu
Margit Buba Antauer
Margot Grimwood
Mihai Surubaru
Mike Smith
Mohamed Ghazala
Monster Chang
Nancy Denney-Phelps
Nelson Shin
Nicole Salomon
Noureddin ZarrinKelk
Oscar Desplats
Pencho Kunchev
Raoul Servais
Roland Schutz
Sayoko Kinoshita
Stephen Worth
Tal Barli
Thomas Renoldner
Tsvika Oren
Vesna Dovnikovic
Vivien Halas
Wiola Sowa

EPILOGUE

ASIFA has now arrived through the past 50 years of promoting animation to be one of the mainstays of this wonderful art form. And it all started when a few animation masters from many different countries launched this meaningful organization, ASIFA, in 1960. In order to commemorate our historical activities we hope to have shed new light on the 50 years of our history and we tried to briefly record our activities for the next generation of animation creators in the world.

I would like to express my sincere appreciation to all the people who provided their precious helping hands for completing the book: the chapter members who wrote articles, and searched and offered pictures and drawings, the editing team, especially, the editor-in-chief, Ed Desroches, and all ASIFA Board members who reviewed and commented on the book.

Nelson SHIN
President of ASIFA